Once Upon a Time

My Life with Children's Books

SHEILA EGOFF
with WENDY K. SUTTON

ORCA BOOK PUBLISHERS

National Library of Canada Cataloguing in Publication Data

Egoff, Sheila
Once upon a time: my life with children's books / Sheila Egoff with Wendy K. Sutton.
Includes bibliographical references.

ISBN 1-55143-335-4

1. Egoff, Sheila. 2. Children's librarians--Canada--Biography.

I. Sutton, Wendy K II. Title.

Z720.E47A3 2005   020'.92   C2005-905802-1

First Published in the United States: 2005
Library of Congress Control Number: 2005934041

Summary: Published posthumously, *Once Upon a Time* is Sheila Egoff's own story of her life as one of the world's great experts on Canadian children's literature.

Orca Book Publishers gratefully acknowledges the support for its publishing programs provided by the following agencies: the Government of Canada through the Department of Canadian Heritage's Book Publishing Industry Development Program (BPIDP), the Canada Council for the Arts, and the British Columbia Arts Council.

Cover design and typesetting: Lynn O'Rourke
Cover Image: Getty Images

Orca Book Publishers
PO Box 5626 Station B
Victoria, BC Canada
V8R 6S4

Orca Book Publishers
PO Box 468
Custer, WA USA
98240-0468

www.orcabook.com
Printed and bound in Canada
08 07 06 05 • 4 3 2 1

Acknowledgments

Here I would like to acknowledge assistance with this project from friends and colleagues: Kit Pearson, Kathryn Shoemaker, Wendy Sutton, Maggie de Vries, Judith Saltman and Tracey Wowk.

THE WORKS OF SHEILA EGOFF

The Republic of Childhood:
A Critical Guide to Canadian Children's Literature in English

Only Connect:
Readings on Children's Literature

Notable Canadian Children's Books

The Republic of Childhood (second edition)

One Ocean Touching:
Papers from the first Pacific Rim Conference
on Children's Literature (editor)

Thursday's Child:
Trends and Patterns in Contemporary Children's Literature

Worlds Within:
Children's Fantasy from the Middle Ages to Today

The New Republic of Childhood

Canadian Children's Books: 1799–1939

Only Connect:
Readings on Children's Literature (second edition)

Some Paradoxes to Ponder

Children's Literature

Books That Shaped Our Minds

CONTENTS

Note: All chapter titles for *Once Upon a Time*
are drawn from Robert Louis Stevenson's
A Child's Garden of Verses, a favourite of Sheila.

The quotations that appear at the top of pages
throughout the book are drawn from Sheila's writing.

INTRODUCTION

*T*hose of you who knew Sheila Egoff will understand how saddened I am to be writing this introduction without her collaboration, as this is her story. I will always remember our years of friendship with great affection and gratitude. Sheila was unique in that her life, from the age of eight on, was devoted to and involved with Canadian books and librarianship. Her death on May 22, 2005, created a large vacuum in the world of children's literature and in the lives of the countless people who were influenced by her and came to share her passion for promoting quality in books for young people. Initially she was insistent that this book not be an autobiography, but little by little she conceded that the subtitle, *My Life with Children's Books,* did promise the inclusion of more personal experiences and information than she had initially intended. Slowly at first and then with increasing enthusiasm and comfort, Sheila shared memories of her childhood in Galt, Ontario, her mother and brother, her school days, her varied library duties and experiences, alongside her discussion of the many books that she recalled with pleasure and admiration.

To give readers a fuller picture of Sheila than would be found in her own words, I invited former students, colleagues and friends to write vignettes or recollections about Sheila, stories that she would have been too modest to tell herself. In fact, when I told Sheila of my plan, her only stipulation was that any writing that was overly complimentary not be incorporated into the book. However, as one former student and friend stated, not being complimentary was impossible when writing about Sheila. These voices of longtime friends that comprise the "After Words" chapter provide valuable insights into Sheila, her influence, her generosity and her infectious love of life.

Sheila often favoured a chronological approach in her professional writing, and quite appropriately that is the structure of this memoir. She continued to be true to a quotation that she enjoyed, borrowed from Lewis Carroll's *Alice's Adventures in Wonderland*: "'Begin at the beginning,' the King said, gravely, 'and go on till you come to the end: then stop.'"

Sheila begins her story by describing her early childhood days, the joy of obtaining her own library card, recollections of her early schooling and memories of the many books she enjoyed as she read her way through the Galt Public Library children's collection. After completing grade thirteen at the Galt Collegiate, Sheila yearned to gain more expertise in library work and moved to Toronto, where she earned her Librarian's Certificate at the Ontario College of Education, University of Toronto. Much to her surprise and delight, when she returned home the following year, she was hired by and put in charge of the children's department of the Galt Public Library. Four years later, Sheila accepted an invitation from the world-renowned Lillian Smith to move to Toronto and be a children's librarian in the Boys and Girls House of the Toronto Public Library.

The next twenty years were work-filled and productive for Sheila. In addition to her library duties at Boys and Girls House, she honed her skills as a storyteller, read every book in the children's collection and did live storytelling for the Canadian Broadcasting Corporation's school programs and Sunday family hour. Despite all the demands of her profession, Sheila continued her education and, after seven years of part-time course work, earned a BA degree from the University of Toronto in 1947. She then obtained a University Diploma in Librarianship at London University and successfully wrote the (British) Library Association examination to become a fellow of the Library Association before returning to the Toronto Public Library in 1948. Four years later, Sheila left Boys and Girls House to work for the next five years at the Toronto Reference Library.

In 1957 Sheila was invited by Elizabeth Morgan to move to Ottawa to join the staff of the Canadian Library Association (CLA). In this new role, her energies were primarily devoted to the Canadian Microfilm Newspaper Project and to serving as an editor on several CLA publications. Sheila spent five years with the CLA. Then, on a typical stifling-hot Ottawa afternoon in 1961, she received a call from Dr. Samuel Rothstein, the director of the new School of Librarianship at the University of British Columbia, and enthusiastically agreed to leave Ottawa and move to Vancouver to join the library school staff. She stayed at UBC for twenty-one years.

Immediately following her official retirement, Sheila was back on the bus to UBC each day, where she devoted over a decade to classifying and annotating the books in the Arkley Collection of Early and Historical Children's Literature. The two unique catalogues that culminated her work were just a portion of the impressive body of professional writing that she accomplished following her retirement until her failing vision limited her ability to read and do research. Sheila's impressive "second" career was filled with honours, such as the prestigious Order of Canada, honorary doctoral degrees and significant awards and recognition from around the world for her scholarly publications and her advocacy of quality books for children.

This memoir ends with a chapter in which Sheila revisits a number of the areas of reading, children's literature and librarianship about which she had strong convictions and a number of serious reservations.

I am confident that when librarians, teachers, parents and the creators of books for the young read about the accomplishments and contributions of this remarkable person, they will recognize the priceless legacy that Sheila Agnes Egoff has left to them and to the children in their care.

Wendy K. Sutton

CHAPTER ONE

That Enchanted Ground

$\mathcal{M}$y mother, Lucy Joyce Egoff, could never have imagined that the most important thing she did for me would turn out to be sending me to the local public library in our small Ontario city of Galt.

Unfortunately, due to a lack of resources, my older brother George and I did not grow up with books in our home. Even in the Catholic elementary school I attended, reading fiction or, for that matter, reading anything for pleasure was not valued, and there was no school library or librarian. On Friday afternoons, the nuns would read to us as a reward for the week's work, but they always chose short, didactic religious stories such as "The Little Lady of the Snows." As a consequence, I was not an eager early reader. In the 1920s there were no kindergartens in Galt (now Cambridge), and when I began school in grade one, I had not learned to read. I came home weeping after my first day and told my mother that the teacher had written something on the board, and I had not recognized it as my name. I was particularly upset because my younger cousin, Catherine Murray, had proudly read out her name when it was written on the blackboard.

My mother sat me down that minute and taught me the alphabet in one evening. For all practical purposes, I was reading the next day. She gave me the code, and I was soon ready and able to apply it. Many modern parents are keen to have their children read as soon as possible, and I agree that reading easily and well is important. But reading readiness is a necessary component: by grade one I was more than ready.

I feel I should provide a little personal history at this point. My father, Dane Egoff, had been a shoe designer in Bulgaria and, because of the shoe factories, had come to Galt where he met and later married my mother. They moved to Auburn, Maine, where I was born in 1918. Tragically, my father drowned in a swimming accident in 1920, and my mother, George and I returned to Galt, where my mother soon remarried.

Our family house was built in the early 1850s, and I learned recently, much to my surprise, that it has been declared a heritage home. It was a duplex with no hot water and no bathroom except for a toilet. We had an inside pump by the sink but had to heat our water for cooking, laundry and bathing. From the kitchen, a trapdoor opened to stairs down to the cellar where we kept an icebox and coal for heating. I learned more about the house, 110/112 Wellington Street, from information provided by the Cambridge Archives and Cambridge Municipal Heritage Advisory Committee and published in the *Cambridge Times*. Described as an Ontario Gothic-style design, popular across the province from 1850 to 1870, this house could date back as far as 1851, making it older than the first city hall. The house is described as architecturally unique because, rather than being a single-family home, it is a semi-detached duplex constructed of painted brick. I wish my brother George were alive to share a good laugh with me about the special attention our old home, a house that neither of us particularly loved, is now receiving

Around 1939, as I remember that I was working full-time, we got our first telephone. The first time it rang, a girl was on the line asking for George. Mother warned me, "Don't ever let me catch *you* phoning up a boy!" Actually, although I had some experience answering the telephone at the Galt Public Library, I was never comfortable using it.

Born in Bally Bay, Ireland, in 1891, my mother never had a paid job until after World War II began and she started working in a munitions factory in Galt. She liked working there and enjoyed the independence that earning money gave her. I remember that when she received her first paycheque, she spent most of it on clothes for me. Then we celebrated by having Boston cream pie at the Chinese restaurant.

Despite her delay in teaching me to read, my mother was a great reader herself, chiefly of what I later came to know as "romantic novels." She was also very shy, so when I turned eight in 1926, she decided that I was old enough and reliable enough to go to the library on her behalf. Down I went to the riverfront, and up the stairs I climbed to the front door of a formidable redbrick building. Once inside, I made my way up another flight of stairs to the main floor. I later learned that this intimidating building, the typical style of a monument to knowledge and to Andrew Carnegie, was also designed to serve as a protection against the periodic flooding of the Grand River. I approached a long wooden desk and handed my mother's book request and her library card to the person standing on the other side. While waiting, I looked around and found myself in a huge room filled with elderly men reading newspapers. Of more interest to me was yet another staircase, at the top of which were two signs: one sign read "Children's Library" and another read "Shhh." The latter had been amended with the addition of "it." A boy, I thought to myself disdainfully.

After I collected my mother's books, I went up that tempting staircase and stepped through the doorway to discover one of the most beautiful rooms I had ever seen. Sunlight poured through large windows overlooking the river. Gaily coloured material curtained those and the windows of another wall; the remaining two walls were covered with shelves of books, and a long central table was strewn with magazines. I paused in the doorway, spellbound. I had no idea that twelve years later I would be in charge of that magnificent room. Seeing me standing in the doorway, a friendly woman approached and asked if I needed any assistance. When she realized that this was my first visit, she gave me an application for a library card—my very own library card!—to take home for my mother to sign.

The next day I was waiting outside the library at opening time with my signed application. I selected a book for myself, likely the Grimms' fairy tales, and could not wait to start reading it. I turned to the first page on the way out of the library and finished the book while walking home. I turned right around and went back to the library for another book. But the now not-so-friendly woman would not give me another one, likely because, as I learned years later, doing so would have spoiled their circulation records. I was informed that I could borrow only one fiction and one non-fiction book a day.

Disappointed, I reread the same book during my second trip home that day and discovered, to my delight, that I enjoyed it even more. I have been a great rereader ever since. Not surprisingly, I continued to read fairy tales: Hans Christian Andersen, the Andrew Lang coloured fairy-tale books and certainly more books by the Brothers Grimm. Then I discovered fairy tales with the word "Canadian" in the title: *Canadian Wonder Tales* and *Canadian Fairy Tales* by Cyrus Macmillan. These collections were my first introduction to our First Nations legends, and I loved them. For many years these two books were Canadian children's only access to such stories. Each was beautifully bound and illustrated in soft colours with the characters dressed in fairy-tale-like costumes.

Decades later I realized that the Cyrus Macmillan retellings were not considered as authentic as those by the retellers of the 1960s, as Macmillan's versions tended to be too romanticized, but I have never forgotten those lovely books, especially the story of "The Indian

Cinderella." I must have read it at least seven times. I believed that seven was a magic number, so I always read an especially good book seven or more times. Macmillan's version of the Cinderella story had the general structure of the classic Perrault retelling, and for the first time I realized that a story could have the same plot but take place in different settings and cultures. Ever since that discovery, I have been intrigued by different versions of the same story. Noticing my interest in First Nations legends, the children's librarian in Galt gave me a book by a young woman from Ontario called Pauline Johnson, who had a Mohawk father and an English mother. I devoured Johnson's *Legends of Vancouver*, a rather shabby-looking little book filled with wonderful stories including "The Two Sisters," "Siwash Rock," "Point Grey," "The Lure of Stanley Park" and "A Royal Mohawk Chief."

The collection of the children's library into which I happily wandered in 1926 set the standard for my future philosophy of children's librarianship. In the 1920s, few books for children were being published in Canada, but many were pouring into the country from the United States, particularly those commercial series of scant literary or inspirational value such as the Tom Swift books, the Radio Boys, the Radio Girls, the Campfire Boys and the Campfire Girls. The librarian of the Galt Public Library children's room stocked none of these. A child who wanted to borrow books from the library's collection had but one choice: to read something worthwhile. Except for a few American classics such as *The Adventures of Tom Sawyer, The Adventures of Huckleberry Finn* and *Little Women,* and a few notable Canadian examples, worthwhile books in the English language were primarily being published in Britain. In a collection of only a few thousand books, it did not take me long to find L.M. Montgomery's *Anne of Green Gables*, which I read my customary seven times. I did not enjoy its sequels as much, since I was too young to be interested in Anne as a young woman. I still think Montgomery should have portrayed Anne as a child in more books than she did.

I also found Montgomery's Emily books in this well-run library because they were shelved next to the Anne books. Emily's life paralleled Anne's in many respects, but what impressed me most after reading the three Emily books was Emily's determination to remain a writer even after her marriage, like Montgomery herself, whereas Anne gave up her writing career for the more traditional roles of wife and mother. The Emily books are far more autobiographical than the Anne books. As a child reader, I was greatly impressed with the marriages, the talk about marriages, the deaths and the family quarrels, all of which gave me insights into the adult world, although much was beyond my comprehension.

Many years later, when I was living in Vancouver, I was asked to give a public appraisal of the Emily books, which I did with great delight. I enjoyed rereading the books and worked hard on my speech in which I praised Emily exuberantly while relegating Anne to a lesser status. However, some of my comments were met with hostility from people in the audience who did not approve of anyone criticizing any of Montgomery's titles. I greatly enjoyed Lucy Maud's journals, and I have grown to respect her as a person and as a writer. I had not realized what a stylist Montgomery was until I became immersed in her journals, where her real passions and understanding are revealed. I remember laughing to myself when I read that even she was tired of Anne and had for that reason created a new personality in her book *Emily of New Moon*. I also discovered, when rereading Montgomery, that she excelled in her portrayal of adult characters. She did not hide their foibles or their dark sides from her youthful readers. Oddly enough, the one novel she may have intended for adults, *The Blue Castle*, was not a great success with an older audience, although the Anne aficionados fell on it eagerly.

Since Nellie McClung's books were next to Montgomery's on the library shelves, I soon discovered McClung's *Sowing Seeds in Danny*, although I only came to understand later that the title meant raising Danny, not planting seeds in him. I only discovered many years later

Children are intensely curious, impressionable and avid for experience. In their quest for knowledge and comprehension of the larger world, books have a power to engage their minds that is quite unmatched in later life.

—The Republic of Childhood

that Nellie McClung was one of Canada's first feminists and had served as a Liberal MLA for Edmonton. I thought her little heroine Pearlie Watson was the most unlikable child in children's books. She was always reforming people and spreading sunshine and light wherever she went. Not being that kind of child, I despised her. In fact, I was a rather stolid child with my nose constantly in a book. I did not take much notice of what went on around me and tended to accept people as they were rather than harbouring any interest in changing them. However, I do remember that at the age of twelve, I had a strong desire to attend a Catholic girls' school and go to China to convert the Chinese, a notion that I soon abandoned. Like most young girls, I had many unattainable dreams, such as becoming an opera star (even though I could not sing) and a ballet dancer (despite the fact that I was a pudgy little girl). When I became a teenager, I aspired to be a highly regarded fashion critic, an ambition that I channelled into a lifelong love of stylish clothes.

When I was a child, horse-drawn carriages still travelled the streets of Galt, but I must admit to paying little attention to them. Why I became so full of empathy for Black Beauty, the ill-treated horse in the novel of the same name, I cannot imagine. However, I could not handle the cruelty in the book toward the horse and could not bring myself to reread it. In my visits to the library, I chanced upon many books that I did not realize were Canadian, for example, *Beautiful Joe* by Marshall Saunders. As it was published in the United States, it was generally regarded as an American book. Actually, I would not have wondered whether it was a Canadian book, and frankly, as a child reader, I would not have cared. Here was a moving story similar to *Black Beauty* about an abused animal that manages to overcome the cruelty it experiences. Because I could more easily relate to a dog, the story of *Beautiful Joe* meant more to me and distressed me far more than did the story of a mistreated horse.

At about the same time as I was reading Montgomery and McClung, I discovered adventure stories set in Canada that illustrated the validity of Emily Dickinson's famous line, "There is no frigate like a book/ To take us lands away." My "lands" were my own country, and I became immersed in the world of the Canadian boy-hero, probably because I had started reading the books my brother George brought home from school. Those included many books by British authors, especially those who enjoyed writing about adventures in the Canadian wilderness, particularly in northern Ontario and British Columbia. Often I chose books solely on the basis of the picture on the front cover. I read all of Hugh Walpole's novels. His Jeremy books soon became favourites, as did books by R.M. Ballantyne, especially *The Young Fur Traders*, one of his two books set in Canada and influenced by the six years he worked for the Hudson's Bay Company as a teenager .

Among the few Canadian-authored books I read at that time was Norman Duncan's *The Adventures of Billy Topsail*, the story of a poor Newfoundland boy who is rescued from drowning by his dog. It is an incredibly exciting story because the boy misunderstands what his dog is trying to do and struggles against him. The rescue is, for me, the most memorable description in any children's book, from any culture, that I have ever read. Educational authorities also appear to have recognized its merit, as for many years the story was a staple in Canadian children's readers. I did not follow Billy's further adventures, perhaps because I had a preference for books about children, whereas Billy reaches young adulthood and endures what is currently referred to as a "rite of passage" and joins his father's fishing crew. Also reflecting that eastern part of Canada was *Adrift on an Icepan* by Sir Wilfred Grenfell, the story of a young Inuit boy stranded on an icepan and his daring, adventurous return to his nomadic family. It was the first book I had read about the Inuit, and my first glimpse of the dangers and hardships of arctic life. Many years later when I read James Houston's *Tikta'liktak: An Eskimo Legend*, I felt transported back to the world of Dr. Grenfell. I also read *Gold, Gold in Cariboo! A Story of Adventure in British Columbia* by C. Phillipps-Wolley, my first introduction to gold fever in Canada. I was astonished by what the early prospectors endured in order to retrieve a few nuggets of gold, and I often think that my lack of desire to own gold is directly attributable to having read about the prospectors' suffering.

Much to my delight I came across *The Boys of Grand Pre School* by James De Mille of New Brunswick, a Canadian school-story set on the shores of the Maritime provinces. The boys spent their school days sailing around the waters of the Bay of Fundy with an incompetent captain and a black cook. What exhilarating, amusing adventures they had! James De Mille was a professional writer, turning out some twenty-seven books, eleven of them intended for boys, between 1869 and his death in 1880. For the most part these were carefree, insouciant stories of boys' lives recounted in staccato, conversational style and free of didacticism. They displayed none of the schoolboy cruelty or intellectualism that later characterized Kipling's famous *Stalky and Co.* For their time and for Canada they were refreshingly original. De Mille's description of the maritime coast in the Brethren of the White Cross series is as impressive as any Canadian setting found in adult books of this period. I must confess that for years I thought the BOWC was something akin to the infamous Ku Klux Klan in the southern United States and therefore resisted reading most of the series.

The first detective story I read was Erik Kastner's *Emil and the Detectives,* and I have enjoyed mysteries ever since. Later, when I was teaching, *Emil* became my "touchstone" book for children's mysteries. I also particularly enjoyed reading about children who act in concert with one another. Paul Berna's *A Hundred Million Francs* and *The Street Musician*, translated from French, both depicted poor but resourceful children, free of the influence of adults, happily working together to solve a problem.

As with most children, my reading was random, but through it I became familiar with many parts of Canada. For example, a poet named William Drummond from Quebec introduced me to a province hitherto unknown to me. Through his humorous dialect verses depicting Quebec habitant characters, I gained insights into the French-Canadian way of life and the attitude of the Quebecois toward "the English." Although no special title occurs to me, French Canada also became familiar to me through my reading about the *coureurs de bois*, the intrepid runners of the woods, who worked as guides for the explorers. Through my childhood reading I became aware of the important role those men played in the development of the Canadian West and the Northwest.

In my book journeys, I soon came across Charles G.D. Roberts from New Brunswick and Ernest Thompson Seton from Ontario. I had no idea how famous they were; I just knew that I liked the way they wrote about animals. Seton's strong simple sentences and Roberts's more poetic and flowery style first alerted me to distinctions and differences in literary style.

Not only did these two authors open my urban, small-town eyes to the world of wild animals, but they also revolutionized the animal-story genre around the world. In the early twentieth century, their writing made a considerable contribution to world literature. Prior to them, the general pattern of the animal story had long since strayed from what must have been its origin: a primitive hunter relating his escape or describing his kill to an admiring group of friends and family, likely colouring the account a bit, but generally recounting the animal's actions realistically. Later, this primeval relationship between man and animal became shrouded in mythology and legend, and the denizens of forest and field, sky and water were used mainly to illustrate a moral for the benefit of humankind. In place of the moralizing and sentimentality of their predecessors, Seton and Roberts substituted a rigorous naturalism, even though touches of anthropomorphism are apparent. They were interested in their animal subjects as animals, not as didactic literary devices. They assumed that their animal heroes were as worthy of interest as any human being, and they created a new form—the animal biography. As biographers do, they undertook an analysis of character based on the influence of environment, youthful training and education, with a selection of facts and events to make the portrait emerge more clearly. Because Seton and Roberts were frequently so specific about the death of animals in the wild, I have found myself with some sympathy for the concept of housing wild animals in zoos. As Seton put it, the life of a wild animal always ends in tragedy. And using his poetic skills, Roberts wrote, "and death stalks joy forever among the kindred of the wild." I am surprised and disappointed that so few novels and short stories in this genre are being written today. Canada introduced this genre to the world but appears to have lost interest in it. We do have nature magazines and factual narratives, but their accounts are brief while our skies, forests, rivers and oceans are still filled with wild life, each creature with a story deserving to be told.

One story of the backwoods of Ontario, Catharine Parr Traill's *Canadian Crusoes: A Tale of the Rice Lake Plains*, particularly delighted me because for once the protagonist was a young woman rather than a young male. The heroine seemed to me both more caring and more daring than the boys did. She is also the one who shows the most empathy toward the abused First Nations girl whom they meet and manage to save. I still remember the shock of the ending, when after enduring three years in the wilderness the young people discover that they had been only seven miles from their homes. *Roughing It in the*

Bush, Canada's great story of pioneer life by Catharine's sister, Susanna Moodie, is the true story of her family and their experiences in Ontario. The description of her life gave me my first glimpse of the hardships that the early pioneer women endured. Strong mothers have become a staple of modern fiction, but few match the courage and tenacity of Susanna Moodie. In 2004, I was delighted to discover *Catharine Parr Traill: Backwoods Pioneer* by Carol Martin and *Susanna's Quill* by Julie Johnston, two well-written and carefully researched children's books that describe the early-nineteenth-century childhoods of pioneers Catharine and Susanna Strickland.

Set closer to where I lived was *Glengarry School Days*, the collection of homely tales by Ralph Connor (the pseudonym of Rev. Charles W. Gordon). It was such fun to read about school life not that different from my own, with its spelling bees, lessons, school rivalries and jealousies all presented with strong doses of morality, which I only swallowed for the duration of the story. There is little in contemporary children's literature to match these early tales for sheer adventure and for illuminating the lives of the early pioneers who contributed so much to our Canadian way of life.

All through my elementary-school years, I read British and American children's classics such as *Alice's Adventures in Wonderland*, *The Wind in the Willows*, *A Little Princess*, *Tom Sawyer*, *The Wizard of Oz* and *Little Women*. I am sure I read each of them my requisite seven times. I became a veritable speed-reader, devouring almost a book a night. This was easier to do in those years without the distraction of television. My days were full playing Cowboys and Indians, Hide and Seek, a hiding game called Red Light, marbles, jacks and hopscotch with children in the neighbourhood. I was also fond of collecting coloured glass from the glass factory across the street from a friend's home. In the wintertime, we had great fun playing in the snow, usually without snowsuits, making snow angels, building snowmen, having snowball fights, taking sleigh rides, tobogganing and skating on the frozen ponds. Sometimes my friends and I would talk about series books such as the Hardy Boys and the Bobbsey Twins, but after dark most of us were in our own homes, cuddled up with a good book.

I loved school and I loved learning and always tried to meet my teachers' expectations. In fact, I was a veritable goody two-shoes who pleased the nuns by shopping for them every Saturday morning. Although I worked hard at my classes, I am sure many of my grade eight classmates were as surprised as I was when I was awarded the ten-pound gold piece for coming first in the class. There was no denying that I was the nuns' favourite. One of my strongest memories from that time is the astonishment I felt when I learned that the mother of one of the girls in the class had promised to give her a pearl necklace if she came first. No such offer had ever been made to me.

My best friend was Dorothy Jones, who lived down the street from me with her widowed and very protective mother. A wealthy little girl three years younger than I, Dorothy was not permitted to play outside her yard, so to keep her company the neighbourhood children and I used to play at her house. To reward ourselves for having to stay and play there, we would ask for bread and jam each day, which her mother seemed quite willing to provide. Dorothy also had a real playhouse with toys and furniture, which we all enjoyed. If we were alone, Dorothy and I would play dress-ups and movie actresses, but she always got to play the glamorous stars like Joan Crawford, and I always got to be the ugly ones like Bette Davis. My home, her house, her grandparents' house and the playhouse are all still standing in Cambridge. When Dorothy told her grandparents that I did not get any Christmas presents, they gave me a pendant with a ruby-coloured stone. Years later when I was living in a boarding house in Rosedale near Toronto, I was devastated when someone stole the pendant and my mother's engagement ring from my room. Dorothy and I remained friends over the years. When she married, I was her bridesmaid, and when I received the Order of Canada in 1994, Dorothy was the first to telephone to congratulate me. I was saddened to learn that she died in the fall of 2004.

For its time, Alice in Wonderland *was indeed a remark-able book, poking fun at, or parodying, almost every tenet deemed basic by the adults of the time to the rearing of chil-dren. It is almost completely iconoclastic, lacking any sense of morality, religion or respect for adults — even poking fun at the didacticism then prevalent in English children's books.*

—Books That Shaped Our Minds

The children's public library became my home away from home. It had a copy of every kind of book a book-hungry child could want. *Alice's Adventures in Wonderland* was one of my favourites, and when I learned later that it is, after the Bible, the most quoted book in the world, I was not at all surprised. I found it easy to accept that Alice grew shorter one moment and taller the next. Today I can still quote from those beloved early children's books such as *Alice* and *The Wind in the Willows*. "Off with his head!" and "Oh bother, oh blow... Oh hang spring cleaning."

I am not sure when I first read Frances Hodgson Burnett's *The Secret Garden*, but I read it frequently and became a great admirer of the heroine, Mary, who begins the story as a far-from-pleasant child. I used to imitate her sour expressions until my mother would tell me to stop clowning around and get my homework done. Unfortunately I could not make myself skinny like Mary as there was too much food around the house. But what a relief to be away from goody-goody child characters such as McClung's Pearlie Watson, Eleanor H. Porter's Pollyanna and Martha Finley's Elsie Dinsmore. I also enjoyed Burnett's *A Little Princess*, a story about cruelty that has what all children's books should have, the comfort of a satisfying resolu-tion. Burnett's later novel *Little Lord Fauntleroy* surprised me with its discussion of democracy, which was unusual in a children's book, but the most memorable aspect of the book were the illustrations by Reginald Bathurst Birch. Every boy must have hated this book as it inspired parents to have their sons wear Little Lord Fauntleroy suits and hairstyles. *Little Lord Fauntleroy* gave me my first exposure to the different political and class systems that existed in other countries, in this case the United States and Britain, and I became more interested in the setting and background of the story than in the character himself.

I am sure that I must have read *Heidi* by Johanna Spyri my usual seven times. Before reading *Heidi* I had never realized the strength of the bond that could exist between the old and the young. I loved Heidi's goats, her love for her grandfather and the memorable alpine ambience. Each day on my way home from high school, I visited my grandmother and read her a serialized story from the *Catholic Record*, but I never felt the intimacy apparent between Heidi and her grandfather. My Scottish grandmother was a stern woman and a strong supporter of Mary, Queen of Scots. One day when I casually remarked that I thought Queen Elizabeth was "really not that bad," my grandmother took me by the ear and put me out of the house.

I sped through the Greek myths, and the Arthurian legends became special favourites, causing me to weep copiously over the death of Arthur. The library copy of Sidney Lanier's *The Boy's King Arthur* had haunting, dramatic illustrations, which I later learned were by the renowned N.C. Wyeth. My reading also included such boys' classics as *Coral Island, Swiss Family Robinson* and, a special favourite, Stevenson's *Treasure Island*. I loved its vivid descriptions of mutiny, piracy and buried treasure and was all ready with pad and pencil to find the treasure myself. I can still quote the second paragraph of *Treasure Island* in which Jim Hawkins describes his first sighting of Billy Bones:

I remember him as if it were yesterday, as he came plodding to the inn door, his sea-chest following behind him in a hand barrow—a tall, strong, heavy, nut-brown man, his tarry pigtail falling over the shoulder of his soiled blue coat, his hands ragged and scarred, with black, broken nails, and the sabre cut across one cheek, a dirty, livid white. I remember him looking round the cove and whistling to himself as he did so, and then breaking out in that old sea-song that he sang so often afterwards: "Fifteen men on a dead man's chest—Yo-ho-ho, and a bottle of rum!"

Louisa May Alcott's *Little Women* became another favourite, mostly because it drew my tears. How I cried over the death of Beth! I am sure the meaning of the American Civil War escaped me, but each of the girls, especially Jo, was completely alive to me. I enjoyed John Bunyan's *Pilgrim's Progress* for its giants and magic and lovely new words and names such as Beelzebub, Delectable Mountains and Giant Despair and his wife, Diffidence. I also appreciated *Pilgrim's Progress* because Edith Nesbit's child characters played at being Pilgrims. It is a tribute to her books that as a fairly young child I knew her last name and wanted to read every one of her books. I am still a Nesbit fan, especially since I can now fully appreciate her special type of magic—magic entering the real world—that characterized her writing long before the present trend of combining fantasy and reality.

I see now that many of the books I read as a child crossed the border between childhood and adulthood, and in those days no one spoke of young adulthood or the young adult novel. Recently at Christmastime, I went to Kidsbooks in Vancouver to get some books for my great-niece and great-nephew, both of whom were approaching adulthood and not keen readers of fiction. When I mentioned their ages, the very capable bookstore owner, Phyllis Simon, recommended books by Agatha Christie to bridge the gap that often exists between children's and adults' reading interests. I was surprised, but upon reflection I understood why. Christie's novels offer much more than a storyline. Her plots are always fast moving, truly "page-turners," but she also provides factual, often useful, details such as how to use the British train system, how to behave during a weekend at a country estate and the value of being alert and observant. When I was preparing to go to England to study for my librarian certificate, I told friends that they need not worry: If I were lucky enough to be invited to a manor house for a weekend, I would know exactly how to behave, thanks to Agatha Christie's books. In their own way, Christie's novels provide insights into the lives and aspirations of other people, one of the most important things reading can do for us.

Rhythmic verses such as Stevenson's *A Child's Garden of Verses* and A.A. Milne's *Now We Are Six* also appealed to me. Even though I was long past six, I enjoyed the beat and the rhythm of the verses. It was my stepfather who set me to memorizing poetry, and I must say that I did not resent it. In school we only memorized individual verses and rarely an entire poem, whereas my stepfather had me memorize whole poems such as Milton's "On His Blindness" and Edgar Allan Poe's "The Raven."

At the end of grade eight, I prepared to leave elementary school. Galt was the centre of the shoe industry, and cotton and linen mills lined the banks of the Grand River. Although all my classmates left school to work in the mills, my mother was insistent that I further my education. She had hopes for my future and was most anxious that I not end up as a mill worker. Also in those days, once you left elementary school you were entitled to an adult library card, so I left my childhood library and moved downstairs to the adult department. For some time I did not feel as at home there as I had among the wonderful children's collection, but I soon came to appreciate the advantages of the adult collection as I moved on to the next stage of my education and reading.

Where Shall We Adventure?

*L*eaving a small Catholic elementary school for a large public high school was indeed a rite of passage. Fortunately I adapted quickly, having a chameleon-like quality to my nature. I soon located the library, which I later realized must have been one of the best high school libraries, if not the best, in Canada at the time. One of the reasons for its excellence was Miss Margaret Fraser, a professional school librarian imported from the United States, who dedicated all her energies to working with both teachers and students. I remember that she refused to teach a subject class as she believed her role as librarian was to serve the entire school and to be in the library at all times.

The library, a huge room packed with free reading and curriculum texts, operated on an open library system that enabled students to work with the collection anytime during the school day. It also served as the study and detention hall. A library that was available to students throughout the school day was most impressive for its time, especially as, decades later, many schools still limit access to the library during school hours to individual classes at prescribed times.

It was probably inevitable that the next wave would be one of sentimentality, sparked by the general late Victorian and Edwardian idealism of the child and reaching its best in Robert Louis Stevenson's A Child's Garden of Verses. *Well into the twentieth century, almost every book of verse for children in the English-speaking world was an echo of Stevenson.* —Books That Shaped Our Minds

I was most impressed with Miss Fraser and decided that being a librarian must be the most wonderful job in the world.

For the first two years of high school, Canadian books were not part of my reading; instead I was immersed in Greek and Roman ancient history, European history and English literature. Then, when I was sixteen, Miss Fraser recommended I be hired as a page to shelve books at the Galt Public Library. I had some experience already helping in the school library, but now I earned twenty-five cents an hour for two hours after school, five days a week. I considered it a privilege to be working in a public library, and I can still recall the pleasure and sense of independence I experienced when I used my first earnings to buy a white satin blouse that I had been yearning for. It cost me two dollars.

Oh, the joys of messing about with books, but woe betide me if I misshelved one of them! The chief librarian, Miss Moyer, had impeccable taste in literature and generously shared her insights with this shy high school student. Under her influence, I discovered the poetry and essay sections in addition to the impressively long shelves of fiction. The Galt library had an outstanding staff of professionally trained librarians who made every effort to bring in the newest and best books available. It was an important and rewarding training experience for me. Inevitably, I came across Stephen Leacock, the man who jumped on a horse and rode madly off in all directions at once, and the man who in the 1930s was already known as our greatest humourist. When the CBC named one of its shows *Madly Off in All Directions*, I was furious that I had not thought of the name myself, but I was even more upset that they do not credit Stephen Leacock when they use the phrase.

Peter McArthur was another Canadian essayist I enjoyed, not for his serious works but for his early works about Ontario's rural countryside. I still wonder why, as an urban child, I was enthralled with all this Ontario rural nostalgia, but I was. After all, I did not live in early Roman times either, but one day the school librarian caught me down in Galt's Soper Park reading *The Decline and Fall of the Roman Empire*.

However, it was the poetry section that most attracted me. I remember a whole row of books of Canadian poetry, some rather battered but readable, and I instantly took to them and have loved poetry ever since. I must confess that because of my early reading of Canadian poetry I still prefer poetry that rhymes. I have nothing against modern poetry *per se*, although I think it was e.e. cummings who caused me to give it up. For me, most of it read more like prose than poetry, and I was a teenager wanting rhythm and rhyme. Rhyme helps you remember a poem, and what good is poetry if you are unable to recall it, especially in the middle of the night when you are finding it difficult to sleep? Canadian poetry also felt familiar because I had read the poems of Pauline Johnson as a child. Her poetry's steady beat, such as in "The Song My Paddle Sings," was perfect for an impressionable high school student. I can still recite:

> August is laughing across the sky,
> Laughing while paddle, canoe and I,
> Dip dip where the hills uplift
> On either side of the current swift.

One of my most-treasured possessions is the 1913 edition of *The Oxford Book of Canadian Verse* edited by Wilfred Campbell. I find that I remember poetry that has strong rhythm and rhyme, vivid images and pleasing content, such as Archibald Lampman's "A January Morning":

> The glittering roofs are still with frost; each worn
> Black chimney builds into the quiet sky.

What Ontario child wouldn't know about winter? And then Sir Charles G.D. Roberts' "The Tantramar Revisited":

> Summers and summers have come,
>   and gone with the flight of the swallow;
> Sunshine and thunder have been, storm,
>   and winter, and frost.

And this from Marjorie Pickthall's "Quiet":

> Come not the earliest petal here, but only
> Wind, cloud, and star,
> Lovely and far,
> Make it less lonely.

Later I discovered and read Isabella Valancy Crawford because I was attracted by her name.

During my time in the Galt Public Library, I also had to shelve books in the children's department, where I felt very much at home. While there I came across a book by Grey Owl (Archibald Stansfeld Belaney) titled *The Adventures of Sajo and her Beaver People*. Unable to resist a title with the word "adventure" in it, I eagerly read this book and still regard it as one of my favourite Canadian children's books. I find it difficult to understand why it is not considered a Canadian classic as it has everything going for it.

Every book that a child reads comes to him only after a decision about it has been made by an adult, or, more exactly, by many adults: writer, publisher, bookseller, librarian, parent and/or teacher... It is children, however, who make the final decision about what is lasting... The children of the next generation will show us whether we have been right about the books we favour now.

—The Republic of Childhood

Although Canada has excelled at the naturalistic animal story, *The Adventures of Sajo and her Beaver People* is one of the few books that shows a mystical bonding between child and animal and has a happy, environmentally satisfying ending. As a First Nations child, Sajo knows that the little beavers must be returned to their natural habitat. When I discovered that the author, Grey Owl, was a white man, I was only upset for a short while because he appeared to have the sensitivity and concern for the universe and its creatures that I had always associated with First Nations cultures.

During my four years as a library page, I explored the fiction section and continued to find myself attracted to material about my own country. I discovered Frederick Philip Grove and such books as *Our Daily Bread* and *A Search for America*, in which he graphically describes his life in Canada and the United States as an immigrant and itinerant labourer. I also read all seven books of Mazo de la Roche's Jalna series about the Whiteoaks family. I loved the Ontario backgrounds, and the series helped me gain insight into a family other than my own.

I also learned to love magazines. These were not really childish or even childlike. There was of course the famous American *St. Nicholas* magazine, which published many of the great American children's books in serial form, such as *Hans Brinker* by Mary

Mapes Dodge. And there were the English school magazines such as *Boy's Own Paper* and *Girl's Own Paper*. How I dreamed of going to an English boarding school! But there were also magazines to stretch one's mind and provide a sense of the world, such as *National Geographic*. My favourite was the *British Illustrated London News*, in whose pages I learned all about British royalty, society women and handsome men.

Perhaps my most memorable reading experience after I began high school was Louis Hémon's *Maria Chapdelaine*, which I know I read at least seven times. Initially I was attracted to it because of the French title, as at that time I had just started compulsory courses in French at the Galt Collegiate. I had expected to be reading a book about the French upper classes, but to my amazement I landed in the backwoods of the province of Quebec. The beginning of the book is not gripping for a youthful reader—elderly men come out of a Quebec village church, light up their pipes, and stand and talk. However, by that time I had learned to skip sentences in my reading and just moved on until Maria appeared and transformed the story. For me, she was the epitome of perfection—beautiful, kind and in love with her province. She even turned down an offer of marriage and a comfortable life in New York. Instead she chose the harsher life of her parents in her native province. Being a selfish teenager, I was astonished that anyone could make such a sacrifice. Hémon's writing has a quality of oral storytelling, moving smoothly from incident to incident at a level that is accessible to a young person. Also, with its Quebecois background, the novel was my first introduction to life in Quebec. I reread it many years later and still enjoyed it and consider it to be a Canadian classic.

I suppose it was predictable that I should come upon E. J. Pratt's *The Titanic* because it received so much publicity when it first appeared. After reading this lengthy narrative poem, I had no interest in seeing the movie or reading subsequent books on the subject as I felt that Pratt had masterfully said it all.

I have always loved history, and the few Canadian historical novels I managed to find opened my eyes to new aspects of my own country. Sir Gilbert Parker's *The Seats of the Mighty*, a novel about the American Revolution, was an unusual book in Canadian literature because it vividly describes the conquest of Canada. I was fascinated as I had never read in my English-language history books about the Plains of Abraham. *The Seats of the Mighty* deals with the battles on the Plains of Abraham and is based upon the published *Memoirs* of Robert Stobo. William Kirby's novel *The Golden Dog* draws upon the same source and details the adventures of a British army spy, Robert Moray, as it vigorously sums up the imperialist view of Quebec's role in Canada. These two books were as romantic as they were informative and gave me a strong sense of *la belle province*, a part of my country that I never tired of reading about. John Richardson's *Wacousta*, a complicated story of the Indian wars of the 1700s, and the first novel written by a native-born Canadian, also intrigued me as a teenager, all 457 pages of it in small type.

Other books I recall from that time include *Kristin Lavransdatter* by Sigrid Undset, and the novels of Sweden's Selma Lagerlöf, the first woman to win, in 1909, the Nobel Prize for Literature. I loved every word of her books and the insights they provided of another culture living in Canada. For the same reason, I remember enjoying *The Viking Heart* by Laura Goodman Salverson, a family saga delineating the Icelandic experience in Manitoba.

It so happened that all my reading of Canadian literature came to fruition for me in a most unexpected way. As I did not have enough money in 1937 to go to university after completing high school, friends suggested that I go to library school in Toronto. In those days the University of Toronto had a diploma program in librarianship as well as a graduate program, neither of which required a university degree. However, as I had just graduated from high school, I was warned that I might not be able to pass the course in Canadian literature that all students were expected to take, whether for a diploma or a degree.

Miss Moyer, the chief librarian of the Galt library, was also a part-time
lecturer at the University of Toronto, and she assured the powers that
be at the library school that I knew more about Canadian literature
than most university graduates. This happily proved to be true. I had
problems with cataloguing and classification, but not with the study
of Canadian literature. I had to move to Toronto for the program and
shared a room in a residence in St. Joseph's College. Unfortunately
my well-to-do roommate resented the fact that I worked so hard. To
keep the peace, I would get up early each morning and look for an
empty classroom to work in.

The greatest thing about the diploma program was the weekly
lecture from Miss Lillian Smith, then head of the world-renowned
children's department of the Toronto Public Library. Miss Smith
had a deep knowledge of literature and an infectious enthusiasm for
children's librarianship. She also had a captivating way of express-
ing herself and excited us with the thought of what we would gain
from working with children and engaging them with books. She
possessed an inspirational quality that made us feel that being a
children's librarian was the most important and rewarding profession
in the world. I enjoyed my courses and instructors and obtained my
Librarian's Certificate in 1938 from the Ontario College of Education,
University of Toronto.

Getting to attend library school was a small miracle for me, but
then an even greater miracle occurred. I returned from Toronto and
not only got a job, but got a job in my own hometown at the Galt
Public Library. Jobs were scarce in 1938, and hardly anyone in my
graduation class was able to get a library position. Yet there I was at
twenty, during the Great Depression, with a full-time library position and important responsibilities. I was in complete charge of the
children's department, but also had to take my turn on the adult
department desk in the downstairs area. The children's collection
soon became a priority in my life.

When I returned home from library school, I was determined to run the children's department in the Galt Public Library just the way Lillian Smith ran Boys and Girls House in the Toronto Public Library, an ambitious undertaking for a one-person operation. I also was determined to discard any book that Lillian Smith had criticized. Among those I removed, I remember in particular the Thornton Burgess books—those sweet little anthropomorphic animal stories, such as *The Adventures of Prickly Porky* and *The Adventures of Chatterer the Red Squirrel.* Out they went, much to the dismay of the children who enjoyed them.

Although I did not rearrange the collection, which was organized by the Dewey Decimal System, my buying policies matched those of the Toronto Public Library. When I found a book for children I thought was first-rate, I bought a set of six so that several children could get the same book at the same time. Multiple copies helped to create a commonality in children's reading and encouraged discussion. Children were able to talk about the books with others older and younger than themselves, much like members of a family sharing their reading experiences.

This multiple-copy approach also supported book talks, which I began to introduce into the elementary schools. I would load up a taxi with books, and off I would go for the morning because I had to be back and on duty at the library around lunchtime. Just as in Toronto, these visits proved to be very successful as they helped to get children excited about quality books. After school, the children from whatever school I had just visited would pour into the library to ask for the books that I had talked about that morning. I cannot remember the titles of the books that I introduced to the children in the Galt library and the elementary schools, but they were popular choices—often books that I had read as a child, and always books that I felt were worthwhile. The teachers were most welcoming, chiefly because in those days there were no school libraries or librarians in the Galt elementary schools. Few children's books had been published at that time, and those that were available had to be used again and again. I confirmed what I had discovered in Toronto: If you were enthusiastic about a book and chose the right part to read aloud, the book sessions with children generated the hoped-for interest in reading.

Across the hall from the children's department was another huge room filled with chairs that I think was intended to serve as an assembly hall but was never used. I took it over for the large groups of one hundred or so youngsters who crowded the library after school. I had a stage constructed for puppet plays and a huge white shadow screen made for performing folktales, First Nations' legends and comic British skits. Many storytelling sessions were also held there, but unfortunately I had to do all of the children's programs myself. The various programs proved to be wonderfully successful, and everyone who participated had a good time. However, they also often meant twelve-hour workdays, as I was regularly on duty alone in the adult department until 9:00 PM.

Then I would lock up the building, after having checked to make certain that everyone was out of the library. Feeling rather nervous about walking home alone, I would have my mother and our dog Aussie, short for Jane Austen, come and walk home with me after I had closed the library. During my years at the Galt library, I started taking night classes at McMaster University for a BA degree, which entailed getting a ride the twenty-five miles to Hamilton once a week.

I went down with a group of teachers who were also working on their degrees. I enjoyed the evenings very much, although I found it difficult to get my homework done because of my many library duties. I liked all of my classes and lecturers, but I particularly appreciated my knowledgeable professor of Canadian history. I remember the lights going out during class, which happened rather frequently, and being most impressed that he was able to continue lecturing without his notes. His classes had such an impact upon me that after completing my BA many years later, I started to work on an MA in history. Unfortunately, I had to give it up because I could not do the coursework justice while working full-time

At the Galt Public Library, I was also responsible for some work with adults, such as giving book talks to groups like the Women's Institute. These women were very keen on books and often wanted librarians to come and talk to them. By this time World War II had begun, and I recall introducing books dealing with the war—not the huge battles and campaigns, but more personal experiences, which those listening seemed to enjoy. On one occasion I really caused a commotion. I had chosen to read from a book about the Queen (Elizabeth II's mother), who was the chief of a particular Canadian regiment, and who at Christmastime had sent plum puddings and a case of liquor to soldiers in the war zone. Well, my presentation to the Women's Institute was to have been followed by a representative of the Salvation Army, who refused to speak because I had mentioned liquor. My unintentional faux pas certainly broke up the meeting.

Like so many young men after the fall of France in 1940, my brother joined the Canadian Army. He was posted to a radar unit in Esquimalt, BC. Around the same time, the Vancouver Public Library advertised for a children's librarian. Almost in fun, I decided to apply for the position with the thought that I would be close to where George was stationed. Then came the Japanese attack on Pearl Harbor, which increased my concern about my brother's safety. I cancelled my application to the Vancouver Public Library, since we Ontarians were convinced that the next stage of the war would involve an invasion by the Japanese through the West Coast of Canada. Such an attack seemed logical to us as western Canada was essentially the breadbasket of the European war effort. We heard reports that the Royal Canadian Navy had escorted ships carrying more than 180,000,000 tons of food and supplies sent to help sustain Great Britain during the war.

I think it was due to my slight acquaintance with Miss Smith and my proximity to Toronto that I was invited to be on an important committee established to form a children's literature association.

Thanks to Lillian Smith, who initiated meetings of children's
librarians across Canada, the Canadian Association of Children's
Librarians (CACL) was established during 1939-40, preceding the
establishment of the Canadian Library Association (CLA) in
1946. The CACL was instrumental in getting a national librarian
appointed for children's librarianship and for establishing the first
Canadian award to be given to the author of a children's book. After
the founding convention of the CLA in Hamilton, the already constituted CACL, feeling that it would be beneficial to belong to the
national organization, requested sectional status, which was granted
at the Vancouver CLA conference in 1947. Also in 1947, the newly
constituted Canadian Library Association founded the Canadian
Children's Book of the Year Prize, to be given for excellence in
writing for children.

Roderick Haig-Brown was the first recipient of the award for his
Starbuck Valley Winter, an excellent choice since before then most
adventure stories read by Canadian children were by British authors
and written mainly for boys. For years I had been reading about bold
and daring boys trudging through the Canadian wilderness, being
kind to First Nations people and conquering animals, but *Starbuck
Valley Winter* gave such literature a new dimension. It had the usual
qualities of male courage and daring, but the hero, Don Morgan,
had a genuine sensitivity for his family, for his environment and
for his friend that was not found in most boys' books of the time.
I believe that Haig-Brown paved the way for other authors of outdoor survival stories, such as Farley Mowat and James Houston, by
introducing characters that were manly but also sensitive.

The CACL is currently a section of the Canadian Association of
Public Libraries and is also part of the CLA. The CACL administers
two important literary awards: The Book of the Year for Children
Award and the Amelia Frances Howard-Gibbon Illustrator's Award,
established by the CACL in 1969.

In purely literary terms, the year 1939 is an important dividing line; it marks the end of an era in writing and publishing for Canadian children. Little appeared during the Second World War and following it, society and its expression, particularly for children, was radically different. —Canadian Children's Books: 1799-1939

In 1942 I was invited by Lillian Smith to join the staff of the Boys and Girls Division of the Toronto Public Library. I am quite sure that the invitation came because librarians were in such short supply during the war. Public librarians were expected to have both a university and a BLS degree, neither of which I had at that time. Perhaps another reason for this opportunity was the fact that Miss Smith loved storytelling. She and I had met again at a CACL conference in Hamilton in 1939, where I had been asked to tell a story. Rather foolishly, I chose Beatrix Potter's *The Tailor of Gloucester* rather than an easier, shorter folktale more appropriate for an amateur to tell. I spent a great deal of time and effort learning the story. I still remember sitting by the kitchen stove night after night, practising, with my mother as my audience. When the time of my storytelling debut came, I froze in the middle of the story. My mind went absolutely blank because, I later realized, my approach to learning the story had been all wrong. However, I did manage to pull myself together and continue. Years later when I was teaching, I understood the difference between learning to tell lore and legend and learning to tell a story that is written in an author's particular idiomatic style, such as that of Rudyard Kipling and, of course, Beatrix Potter. My fast recovery turned out to be more impressive than I could have imagined, and I can still tell *The Tailor of Gloucester* to this day.

Fortunately, Lillian Smith was pleased with my performance, perhaps because the story was rather formidable for a greenhorn to tackle, and perhaps because I had rallied valiantly and successfully. Although the salary was only about a hundred dollars a year more than what I had earned at the Galt Public Library, working at the internationally acclaimed Boys and Girls House with Lillian Smith would offer me valuable training and prestige. Off I went, deciding that I could finish my BA more easily in Toronto than by travelling once a week to Hamilton. I recall borrowing three hundred dollars to pay for moving my furniture from Galt to Toronto, and sharing a room in a house on Huron Street, close to the Toronto Public Library, with Simone, a French-Canadian girl.

CHAPTER THREE
Onward Into Fairy Land

I was looking forward to working at Boys and Girls House, but I was anxious about being on my own. Fortunately the train service between Toronto and Galt was excellent, so I could get home easily on weekends. One time I arrived late and found no mother and dog to meet me. When I got home, the door was open—at that time nobody in town locked their doors—so I went up to my bedroom and found our dog not only asleep on my bed, but under the blankets with its head on the pillow. With Aussie sound asleep in my bed, I had to be content with sleeping on top of the covers. When I complained to my mother, she was not sympathetic. A woman who gave her meat rations to the dog was not going to worry about my weekend sleeping arrangements.

Aussie was a black-and-white springer spaniel that my brother had brought home as a puppy. I can still picture George and his friend Walter carrying into our kitchen two puppies that they had bought at the pound for eight dollars each. Walter was afraid of what his mother would say if he arrived home with a puppy, so my mother stayed up the whole night taking care of them. George and I were

both working at the time, so she volunteered to be the caregiver for
the puppies. She lined a box with a blanket and fed the two of them
with a towel soaked in milk and a bit of brandy, which had mysteriously appeared in our alcohol-free home.

Lillian Smith, head of Boys and Girls House, had trained as a
children's librarian at the Carnegie Public Library in Pittsburgh in
1910, and in 1911 she was hired by Anne Carroll Moore to work
in the children's division of the New York Public Library. In 1912
Miss Smith was appointed director of Children's Services for the
Toronto Public Library and became the first children's librarian in
the British Empire, which meant, of course, that she was the first
children's librarian in Canada as well. Libraries in other provinces
soon followed Toronto's lead. Lillian Smith had dreamed of creating a library designed specifically for children, and in 1922, after a
great deal of hard work and planning, Boys and Girls House was
opened in a renovated Victorian house on Toronto's St. George
Street. In 1926 she opened the first school library in Toronto, another
Canadian first.

Lillian Smith was a charismatic leader and an effective administrator. In fact, I learned a great deal about administration from
working with her. She would always begin with praise when speaking with a member of the library staff and was skillful at identifying individuals' strengths and building upon them. For example, she
remembered that I had a deep interest in Canadian children's books
in addition to storytelling. One year, four or five Canadian children's
books came out simultaneously, which was unusual at the time, and
Miss Smith asked me to review them for the Toronto Public Library
newsletter.

I have to admit that I was not kind in my assessments, and
Miss Smith came charging down the stairs almost in a rage, waving my critiques and exclaiming, "Sheila, you can't do this!" With
some indignation, I replied, "You have always said that we should
judge Canadian books by the same standards that we use to judge

children's books from other countries." "Yes," she retorted, "but you have to temper judgment with mercy." I should have remembered that Miss Smith took a passionate interest in promoting Canadian children's books and authors. For example, she had encouraged Mabel Dunham, then head of the Kitchener Public Library, to write a book about a little Mennonite boy living on a farm near Kitchener. It was called *Kristli's Trees* and was quite charming. She also offered encouragement to Louise Riley, the former head of the children's department of the Calgary Public Library, who wrote a rather unsuccessful book of fantasy called *A Train for Tiger Lily*, which I described in the first edition of *The Republic of Childhood* as "insipid and contrived." But I always have been rather judgmental and have remained firm in my conviction that truth and quality must be valued above all else. If I judge a book to be poor, I spare neither the book nor the author.

During my time at Boys and Girls House, from 1942 to 1952, it continued to be the most famous and respected children's library in the world, with the possible exception of the New York Public Library's children's department under the aegis of Anne Carroll Moore. Lillian Smith's vision for meeting children's reading needs encompassed the entire city of Toronto. We established children's libraries in all the community centres, in the children's hospital, in any school that was more than two miles from a branch library and in schools for the physically and mentally challenged. I doubt that Lillian Smith knowingly overlooked a single child in the Toronto area. Her purchasing policy was to obtain the very best books available. There was to be no giving in to inferior books. She had a trained research staff who identified books they believed merited her attention, and she read every book before it was bought for Boys and Girls House and the branch libraries.

The in-service training program for the children's librarians was another dimension that made Boys and Girls House internationally famous. Experts with specialties such as storytelling or puppetry gave lectures, and time was set aside during daily routines to enable the

*If there are not models of excellence that provide a gen-
uine reading experience for a child—one that catches the
breath, lifts the spirit, or triggers a hearty laugh—then
books are reduced to the merely utilitarian.*

—The Children's Reader (Winter 1998-99)

librarians to attend. The children's collection was open from 9:00 AM
to 6:00 PM, and since there was no need for shift work, a pleasant, collegial atmosphere developed among the staff. Many children's librarians came from the United States and Europe to serve as interns at
Boys and Girls House. In those early days, a children's librarian never
had a desk. We were either out in the schools and community centres
giving book talks or we were assisting children in the branches and
the main library. We literally never sat down. We had library assistants to check out the books while we were busy working with the
children. I cannot recall ever checking out a book in my life. I may
have when I worked in the school library, although my main task
there was to shelve books.

Boys and Girls House was a child-centred library. The organization of books was based on a special alphabetic code invented
by Lillian Smith. She believed that the collection should be organized paralleling the order in which children read. They start with
picturebooks, which were found by their easily recognized "X,"
and then moved up to little children's books, identified by "Z."
From there they advanced to folktales and later to myths and legends, fairy tales, biographies and so on. Naturally, some children
chose their books without assistance, but the most frequently asked
question was, "Can you help me find another book like the one I just
brought back?"

Another aspect of Lillian Smith's administration was to provide new staff members with special training sessions in aspects of children's literature. I remember my sessions with a librarian named Helen Armstrong. Her enthusiasm for, and extensive knowledge of, legends caused us all to fall in love with Arthurian legends. Many years later when I was at UBC, Roy Stokes, the second director of the library school and well aware of my love of legends, approached me a few weeks before the Christmas examinations. "Well, Sheila, have you managed to get past King Arthur yet?" he asked.

What I remember most vividly about my time at Boys and Girls House were the Monday morning staff meetings. The staff gathered for informative talks about children's librarianship rather than merely talks about book selection. Anyone important in children's library work who came to town, either from England or the United States, was invited to speak. But perhaps the most important thing is that we all left the sessions enthusiastic and eager to serve children. Staff were also asked to present papers, tell stories and give book talks at these morning sessions. The children's collection was constantly evaluated as to its content, appeal and accessibility for modern children. I remember our debating whether to keep Bunyan's *Pilgrim's Progress* in the children's department, as it was not being read. We finally decided to keep a very fine abridged version illustrated by Robert Lawson.

Knowing every book in the collection was the mark of a good children's librarian. For example, it was important to know in what order Alexandre Dumas wrote his trilogy *The Three Musketeers*, and whether *Twenty Years After* was written before or after *The Vicomte de Bragelonne*. Storytelling to all ages was also an important part of our library service. We told the Arthurian legends, the Norse and Greek legends, any great story. For the older children, each librarian would learn one story at a time and then travel around to the six library branches on consecutive Saturdays, telling the same story. Consequently, the children heard six different stories over six weeks, and retelling the same story again and again helped us craft our story to near perfection.

Another role we librarians had was to choose books for the CBC to script into radio dramas that were presented every Sunday. The Monday following the broadcast, we waited for the deluge of children eager to get a copy of the book they had listened to on the radio. For several years, I also was involved in live storytelling for the CBC, both for the school broadcast programs and for a Sunday family hour, telling folktales and literary folktales such as Andersen's "The Tinder Box" and "The Nightingale." The Sunday storytelling programs meant that I could not get home to Galt on the weekends, which was a disappointment both to me and to my mother. When my mother visited me in Toronto, Miss Smith finally persuaded her to let me stay to do the programs, saying that it would be good for my career.

Once I had a row with the Toronto Board of Education over my recording of "The Frog Prince" because I refused to substitute a patriotic maple tree for the aspen tree of the original story. I also recall one day when the whole of Toronto was closed down by a snowstorm and I was scheduled to read at the CBC. Unaware that most offices were closed, I struggled through the snow from the edge of Rosedale to the CBC and had to be rescued from the building by friends.

Boys and Girls House attracted many interesting visitors, but perhaps the one I remember most vividly was Anne Carroll Moore, then the retired head of the wonderful New York Public Library Children's Department, who was as influential and eccentric as ever. Her friendship with Lillian Smith made her a frequent visitor to Toronto. Only after many years of research into the history of children's literature did I realize that Anne Carroll Moore was one of the most important people in a long line of influential American women who shaped children's library services as we know them today. These early children's librarians were deeply concerned about children who did not have access to a rich reading environment, and they worked diligently to provide it. Their efforts involved community services and providing books to children in hospitals and disabled children—no child was beyond their reach. They wanted only the best for each child. For example, Caroline M. Hewins, librarian of the Hartford (Connecticut) Library Association, challenged American Library Association members at a conference in 1882 by asking them what was being done in public libraries to encourage a love of good literature among boys and girls.

In the twenty years following Caroline Hewins's challenge, Mary Wright Plummer was among a number of women who championed meeting the reading needs of all children. She believed that children's work was of great importance to the total structure of libraries and developed an appreciation for and interest in such work among many other librarians. Among her students was Anne Carroll Moore, who, in 1906, organized the children's library of the New York Public Library and remained its supervisor until her retirement in 1941.

However, during my time at Boys and Girls House I was only aware of Anne Carroll Moore's eccentricity. She had been given an eight-inch-tall wooden doll she named Nicolas Knickerbocker after the patron saint of the Dutch. I do not know what happened in New York, but in Toronto when Anne Carroll Moore was about to make an appearance, we staff members were asked to stand up and hold lighted candles as a mark of adulation for both woman and doll. As Kipling's elephant's child said, speaking through his nose as it was being pulled by the crocodile, "This is too butch for be," and I made my escape when we were warned of Nicolas's imminent appearance.

Another interesting visitor to Boys and Girls House was the American writer Dorothy Hosford, who enthralled the staff with her knowledge of Norse myths, particularly her retelling of the great epic *Sons of the Volsungs*. Her influence was so great and her storytelling powers so compelling that we instituted a program of telling Norse myths for the children ages nine to twelve, who, I believe, are now overlooked in library storytelling programs. Today most storytelling is tailored for the preschool child or takes place during storytelling festivals mainly intended for adult audiences.

Boys and Girls House was an old Victorian house converted into a children's library. With its special picturebook room and little theatre, working there felt like living in a house furnished only with bookshelves and books. For example, there was no card catalogue. Staff were expected to read and know all the books thoroughly and to talk with children about them.

Every professional librarian in the system was expected to work to that standard and also had to have a specialty, especially in storytelling. For example, Frances Trotter was an expert on the Uncle Remus stories and told them when doing so was not considered politically correct in the United States. Rowen Stock was the acknowledged expert on Hans Christian Andersen, and no new retelling of Andersen was purchased without her approval. Alice Kane was an exceptionally fine storyteller who, with her wonderful Irish lilt, told tales of her native country and became famous in Toronto for creating storytelling gatherings for adults and the Irish. Others were skilled at putting on puppet shows and shadow plays. My specialty was telling English folktales, the more gruesome and bloodthirsty the better. Then there were staff members who had other kinds of expertise, such as Sadie Bush, who was wonderfully effective at supervising the children's libraries in community centres. I remember Sadie as a gentle woman whose first comment to me was, "Do you believe in God?" When she was knocked down by a cyclist, she apologized for being in his way. Judith St. John became famous as the second curator of the Osborne Collection of Early English Children's Books, a gift presented to the Toronto Public Library by Edgar Osborne in recognition of Lillian Smith's enormous contribution to children's librarianship.

In Canada, any children's library worth its salt emulated the Toronto organization and philosophy of Lillian Smith, as I had done when I was the children's librarian in Galt. All children, whether white, black, pink or green, were to be treated equally. This philosophy must have worked because I remember that after 3:30 PM every afternoon, children were lined up at the door, waiting to enter. In those days children's libraries closed at 6:00 PM because children were expected to be at home in the evenings doing their schoolwork. I believe it has been a mistake to keep children's libraries open until 9:00 PM because they are usually staffed by non-professionals or librarians who lack the knowledge of children's collections. For example, I happened to be at a Vancouver branch library once when a child came in after dinner to get some information on bees for a school assignment. The library assistant went immediately to the correct Dewey number on the shelf and told the child that all the books on that subject were out. Apparently he was unaware that many books were available on that subject elsewhere in the library. First of all, there was factual fiction about bees, such as Waldemar Bonsels' *Maya the Bee*. Also, the child could have been taken to the adult department to find some simple material on bees. It greatly distresses me to think that children can be put in a position of receiving little or no skilled assistance when they go to a public library.

After Lillian Smith retired in 1952, the effective but autocratic system that she had established slowly collapsed as children's libraries ceased to be one-person operations.

Miss Smith and her reviewing staff had always made the final decisions regarding collection development, and as a consequence the main library and the branches had the same books. However, since her appointment in 1912 as director of Children's Services, society had changed dramatically, and branch librarians wanted to be free to make their own decisions when ordering material for their particular library clientele.

During World War II, I took evening and summer classes at the University of Toronto and finished my coursework two years after the war ended. It took me seven years to do my BA degree part-time while working at Boys and Girls House and taking only one or two

Myth can now be seen as a dim vision of a reality that our ancestors saw very clearly: the true and fixed nature of things that made for a more orderly world. At their deepest level, myths comprise preliterate humanity's philosophy, religion, history and class structure; at their simplest, they are our ancestors' explanations of natural phenomena. —Books That Shaped Our Minds

classes each year. All the staff members supported me by absorbing some of my library duties and encouraging me to go home and study. In addition to my required courses, I also chose to take Catholic Philosophy and Catholic Logic as elective courses at St. Michael's College, University of Toronto, and the nuns and priests studying there helped explain many aspects of the material. Ironically, and rather embarrassingly, I proved to have excellent exam-taking skills and earned higher marks than those who had been kind enough to assist me.

When I graduated from the University of Toronto in 1947, I was eager for more education in librarianship. On the condition that I find someone to take over my responsibilities, which I did, Miss Smith gave me a leave of absence from Boys and Girls House to enable me to pursue further study. Although I was told that the United States was where librarianship was happening, I went to England, where I could stay with my mother's relatives who lived outside London at Leytonstone, a town at the terminus of the London Underground. My family would have found the American university fees prohibitive, but they were able to send food and clothes to my English relatives to help them deal with the shortages that had been caused by the war.

In the fall of 1947, I flew to New York City to begin my journey to England. After a short visit with my cousin James Murray, who lived in New York, I sailed on the *Queen Elizabeth II*, which had been a troopship during World War II. I remember all the soldiers' names carved into the railings, often coupled with the names of the sweethearts they had left behind. Although I was travelling in steerage, another young woman and I learned how to sneak up to the first-class deck, where our use of the deck chairs was quickly accepted by the stewards. They even brought us the same refreshments as the first-class passengers, but we never managed to make it into the dining room.

I obtained my diploma, the equivalent of a Canadian BLS or MLS, from the London School of Librarianship at London University. A number of our lecturers were experienced, full-time librarians who came to the school after 5:00 PM to teach us. Although I had had five years of Latin and Greek in high school, when I studied paleography, the study of ancient scripts, I was grateful for the help given me by Oxford and Cambridge students in the program. Bibliography, another challenging course not offered at that time in Canada, proved to be of special value to me years later, when, following my retirement from the University of British Columbia, I took on the task of compiling two catalogues of the early children's books housed in UBC's Special Collections. A particularly vivid memory I have of my time at London University is when the Underground broke down as I was on my way to a final examination. I finally managed to get a taxi to the university, but was over an hour late. I remember the concern and kindness of the people on the train and in the station when they learned the reason why I, a total stranger, was so distressed to discover that the Underground was not running. The professor of public librarianship was invigilating the exam, and I recall his advice, which I accepted. "I'm afraid that I cannot do anything for you," he said to me, "but I want you to wait a full twenty minutes before you pick up your pen."

After I completed the University Diploma in Librarianship, I wrote the (British) Library Association examination for the FLA

(Fellow of the Library Association). I learned later that I was one of only two people in Canada who was an FLA, the other being Charles R. Sanderson, chief librarian of the Toronto Public Library and a strong supporter of Lillian Smith and children's librarianship. When I graduated from London University in 1948, I received a visit from Mr. Irwin, the director of the school. "I don't imagine that now you will be going back to Toronto to work with children," he said. I drew myself up stiffly and boldly replied, "I do not believe a person can have too much education to work with children." At that time England had a conservative view of children's librarianship and did not offer a single course in children's literature. My entire education in children's librarianship and literature came from Lillian Smith and my work at Boys and Girls House in Toronto.

While I was in England, and perhaps because I was a Canadian, I was warmly received by the English librarians, and especially by Edgar Osborne, who at that time was head of the Derbyshire Regional Library. Having visited Lillian Smith and Boys and Girls House in 1934, he invited me to his home for a weekend to show me his collection of early English children's books, which he intended to leave in his will to the Toronto Public Library in honour of Lillian Smith. Up I went by train for a weekend visit, not knowing a thing about early children's books. However, I quickly sensed that the collection was very special and knew enough to act suitably impressed, "oohing" and "ahhing" enthusiastically. The books were displayed in elegant glass cases in a beautiful long room with picture windows framing the Derbyshire hills, that stretched off into the distance. In addition to books, Edgar Osborne loved the theatre—his late wife had been an actress—and whenever he came to London for a visit, I made sure that I got tickets for any important plays that were currently running. Apparently my respect for his collection and my hospitality were so appreciated that he decided to give the collection to Toronto right away. He came to Toronto in 1948 to make arrangements, and when the collection arrived a year later I became the first curator of the Osborne Collection of Early English Children's Books. In 1951, Boys and Girls House opened a new Children's Room and Theatre, which left more space in the original building for the Osborne collection, although it is now housed in a new building better suited to its particular needs.

After two years, I decided to become involved in more contemporary librarianship, and the Osborne Collection was taken over by Judith St. John, who remained its curator for many years and made it world famous. Most of the collection consists of first editions, some of which even the British Museum, now the British Library, did not have. The books, all of which are by British authors, range from the seventeenth century to the end of the nineteenth century, three to four thousand volumes in all. The Osborne is one of the most important collections of children's books in the world. If its value had been realized at the time, I believe that the British government would have been unlikely to allow it out of the country.

After completing my studies in London in 1948, I returned to Boys and Girls House and was lucky enough to find an apartment right across from the Toronto Public Library. I had been invited to the continent for a holiday, but when my aunt admitted to me that my mother was very ill, I flew home that June. My well-meaning relatives had kept the news of my mother's illness from me, fearing that it would interrupt my studies. Once I was back in Canada, George dropped me off each morning to be with my mother, but she longed to leave the hospital and died in her sister's home before the end of the year.

Four years later, another great change took place in my career. I awoke one morning and said to myself, "I want to do something new and different." Looking back, I think I was simply very tired. I had had so many years of study and working that I no longer felt energized. I left Boys and Girls House in 1952 and joined the staff of the Toronto Reference Library. The reference work was not particularly challenging, but I enjoyed the stable hours and the opportunity to have a social life with people my own age who shared my interests. Stress disappeared from my professional life. I was now free from preparing book talks and puppet plays, from storytelling, delivering speeches and writing reports.

My work at the Toronto Reference Library resulted in my becoming even more deeply involved with Canadian children's books. In 1952 the reference library, a division of the Toronto Public Library, still provided the bibliographic service of listing and describing all Canadian publications. I was responsible for finding and recording publication data for Canadian children's books, and I remember that for at least two years, no children's books were published in Canada. Many of the difficulties faced by publishers in the early 1950s continue today: a relatively small population scattered across vast distances, small print runs and high printing costs, and a lack of children's book editors and qualified reviewing media.

After I had completed five years of reference work, another great change occurred in my career. In 1957, Elizabeth Morton, the first executive director of the Canadian Library Association, invited me to join the staff at the CLA headquarters in downtown Ottawa. I found an apartment on Laurier Street, a short bus ride to and from the CLA and a block away from Parliament Hill, the Chateau Laurier and the railway station. For five years I continued to be immersed in Canadian literature, working as the supervisor of the Canadian Microfilm Newspaper Project, which I regard as my greatest achievement while at CLA. Night after night I worked at home on the cumulative catalogue, which was formatted on loose-leaf so that it could be more efficiently revised and updated. During my years at CLA, I was also an editor of the *Canadian Periodical Index*, an editor of the *Canadian Library Association Journal*, and co-organizer of a number of related conferences. The demands of all these duties were compounded by the lack of air conditioning to help combat the incredible heat of summer and by the shortage of professional librarians to guide the various projects.

The office had the barest of essentials: one new and one borrowed typewriter, two typing desks, three chairs, a second-hand
table, a bookcase and two dollars' worth of orange crates for shelving.
Although I enjoyed the work and my colleagues, I did not enjoy the
Ottawa climate, which I found to be too hot and humid in summer
and too cold and miserable in winter. Waiting for a bus in minus-
forty-degrees-Fahrenheit weather was not my idea of pleasure.

One of my most challenging responsibilities during those years
was organizing the CLA, ALA and French-Canadian Library
Association (FCLA) conference that was held in Montreal in 1960
and hosted five thousand delegates. Although the ALA had met in
Canada on several occasions, the first in Montreal in 1900, this was
the first joint meeting of the CLA and the ALA since the CLA had
been inaugurated as a national organization. For five months prior to
the conference, I lived in a tiny room in the Laurentian Hotel, long
since gone, and worked with the staff at the new Queen Elizabeth
Hotel, headquarters of the conference. I was in charge of organizing
all the details involved in putting on the large international event. At
the end of what had been a very successful conference, I was invited
by the manager and assistant manager of the hotel to have lunch with
them in the roof garden. I still recall the anger I felt when they presented me with a hotel apron and told me that I should go home and
get married. On the positive side, however, the Montreal conference
prepared me for the task, many years later in May 1976, of organizing
the first Pacific Rim Conference on Children's Literature, which was
held at the University of British Columbia.

Elizabeth Morton was an amazing organizer and a passionate
Canadian. Her two great aims for the Canadian library system were,
first, to remain independent of the ALA and, second but equally
important, to make the French-Canadian organization a full partner
in library development in Canada. The first of her goals was realized,
but not the second as the FCLA became, and still is, independent of
the CLA, in part due to the rise of French-Canadian nationalism.

I have never felt more Canadian than I did during my time in Ottawa. Ottawa was still a very small place in the late 1950s, and as a consequence, those of us interested in Canadian books and literature played an important role, however small. During a cocktail party at one of our literary occasions I met the newly appointed National Librarian, Dr. W. Kaye Lamb, and had the temerity to ask him when he would be appointing a children's literature specialist for the National Library. His eyes bulging with astonishment, he said, "What does the National Library have to do with children's books?" I replied, "They are under copyright!" Then I asked, "What are you going to do with the books? Let them moulder in a basement?" Despite views such as his, the CACL was persistent, and in 1975 one of the greatest librarians Canada has ever produced, Irene Aubrey, was appointed the Children's Literature Librarian/ Consultant for the National Library of Canada. In 1979 the service, employing three permanent staff members, was renamed the Children's Literature Service.

Irene Aubrey always made me think of Pierre Trudeau, as her English was so perfect that one could not believe she was half French-Canadian. From others I came to understand that her French was so good that it was difficult to believe that she was half English. She became an effective ambassador around the world for Canadian children's books and was a strong supporter of all children's librarians in Canada, particularly with regard to their publications, conferences and speeches. Irene Aubrey was strikingly attractive, and I recall her generosity of spirit, her gracious warm manner and her willingness to help whenever and wherever she could. Unfortunately, following her retirement in 1993, no new appointment to an equivalent position was made, which was a great loss for children's librarianship in Canada.

One of my former library-student interns was a parliamentary reporter in Ottawa, and he sometimes invited me to join him for lunch in the House of Commons restaurant. These occasions enabled me to take a few hours off to sit and watch the proceedings in the House, and as a consequence I became very political for a while. In the late 1950s, the CLA decided to present a brief to the government, I think to do with postal rates for books. I took the brief in my hot little hand and trotted up to the House to wait for David Fulton to come out of his meeting so that I could present it to him. He was so rude that I have never forgotten the experience. I should have reminded him not to shoot the messenger, but instead I fled.

In August of 1961, my life and career suddenly seemed to come together. Ottawa was impossibly hot. I had already suffered through the minus-forty-degree winter and now it was over a hundred! On this particular Saturday, I was lying naked on my bed, saying to myself that I must get an air conditioner for my bedroom, not realizing that there probably was not one to be had in the whole city. At this point in my musings, the phone rang and I lazily reached for it. An unfamiliar voice said, "Sheila, this is Sam Rothstein calling from Vancouver." I hastily reached for my housecoat as I was not going to talk in the nude to the prestigious Dr. Rothstein. The voice continued, "Sheila, the temperature out here is seventy-eight, and the Russian Ballet is in town. Why don't you come out and help us start a library school?" I had met Dr. Rothstein at the CLA offices when he was chairperson of an important library committee. We had met again and had a chat at the lobster feast on the beach during the St. Andrews, New Brunswick, conference. My immediate answer to his suggestion was, "I'll be on the next plane." Thinking back, I have to admit that I likely was more interested in getting away from the heat and humidity of Ottawa than I was in establishing a new library school at UBC.

CHAPTER FOUR

By the Side of the Sea

$\mathcal{M}$y career as a university professor began in January 1962 when I arrived in Vancouver to accept an instructor's position at UBC. Dr. Samuel Rothstein had become the first director of the UBC School of Librarianship the previous September, and the first academic year for the School had already begun. At that time, Dr. Rothstein was also the head of the UBC Library and admitted that he often ended up writing letters to himself. I have never driven a car, and Dr. Rothstein graciously drove me around Vancouver in search of a place for me to live. By the end of the first weekend, I found a roomy apartment on Twelfth Avenue just west of Granville Street for a rent of a hundred and fifty dollars a month. The location was wonderful, close to fashionable shops and art galleries and on a bus route to UBC. Twenty years later, I was surprised to learn that the rent for my first Vancouver apartment had risen to seven hundred dollars.

From 1961 to 1970 the UBC library program could be completed in an academic year, seven-and-a-half months, leading to a Bachelor of Library Science (BLS) degree. The interest in the program and the number of applicants were overwhelming as, at the time, people in western Canada hoping to get library degrees had only three choices: the library schools at the University of Toronto or McGill in eastern Canada, or the University of Washington in Seattle. Dr. Rothstein firmly believed that, from its inception, the UBC library school met all the criteria required for accreditation, such as an articulation of its future plans and the quality of the staff and students, and requested that it be accredited by the ALA as early as possible. In January 1963 the ALA accreditation committee enthusiastically commended the school and granted accreditation. His inviting the ALA team during the first year of the program demonstrated the confidence that Sam Rothstein had in both his faculty and the students.

As would be expected, Dr. Rothstein needed to collect a few letters of reference for me. Fortunately, whatever I had already accomplished in my career proved to be to my advantage. He was looking for a librarian with two sets of qualifications. First, he needed a specialist in children's literature, and having a broad knowledge of librarianship himself, he knew that he wanted someone trained at the Toronto Public Library children's department. He also needed an administrative coordinator to help get the program started. Everything had to be planned for—establishing admissions policies, preparing catalogues, vetting and arranging field trips and fieldwork opportunities, recruiting additional faculty members and acquiring all the physical equipment needed to operate a library school. We had spaces for only eighty students, but we interviewed all applicants. I was responsible for processing and preparing the student applications for the interviews, the interview reports, the results of the faculty consultations and the list of students selected. As there were three entry times for admission to the school—September, January and May—these duties were demanding and ongoing.

The fieldwork opportunities alone were very time-consuming as each student had to complete two weeks of fieldwork. These could take place anywhere in Canada, the United States or England; therefore inquiries had to be made and letters of application written. Students also went on field trips to libraries in Vancouver, Victoria and Seattle, for which I made the necessary arrangements, including finding escorts to accompany the students. Fortunately I arrived at UBC with some relevant experience gained from five years of managing conferences and writing and editing at the CLA headquarters in Ottawa.

The administrative duties aside, I still had to design a course in children's literature and build up a teaching collection of books. Although the Toronto library school arranged for lectures once a week from Lillian Smith, neither it nor the McGill library school offered courses in children's librarianship. I became the first full-time university teacher of children's literature in Canada. I was amused by all of this because there I was, once again, back to the beginning of my childhood reading.

The UBC Library had inherited a raggedy collection of children's books from the Victoria Normal School. To my Toronto Public Library sensibilities, the collection was practically useless. I used to steal down to the stacks and simply throw many of the books into the wastebasket, forgetting that the cards for the books were still in the card catalogue. With the rather meagre collection remaining, I could truthfully say that I did not have sufficient children's books with which to teach. I asked for money and was grateful to receive a grant from the Faculty of Education. Today, thanks to the work of many people, the circulating and research collections of children's books at UBC are carefully chosen, extensive and cover all aspects of children's literature. In the beginning, building the collection took a great deal of work because each book had to be separately recorded on an individual order card. Rarely was I able to get home before 11:00 PM.

Eventually I became frustrated with the Main Library's Library of Congress system, as it proved to be a classification nightmare and impractical for the students. By this system, books of the same genre are catalogued and shelved in a number of different places within the children's literature collection. For example, the Library of Congress system has science fiction shelved in six different areas with, for example, short-story collections of science fiction found with short stories. Eventually I asked two of my students to design a new classification system where like book stood with like so that all the books in a particular genre, such as French folktales or English folktales or Canadian folktales, stood together. Some years later this very practical system was destroyed because the cataloguers were only willing to operate with the Library of Congress card that accompanies each book. Schools and public libraries use the Dewey Decimal system, but all university libraries use the Library of Congress system, which admittedly accommodates more breadth of material and can be more easily expanded.

One of the wonderful things about being a member of the faculty of the School of Librarianship was having such interesting colleagues, all of whom took on responsibilities far beyond their teaching roles. In the office next to mine was the cataloguing instructor and our youngest colleague, Dr. Ronald Hagler. He had arrived at UBC a few months before I did, and we were amused to discover that our separate decisions to come to Vancouver were based on the same thing—weather. He had left Ontario because of the cold, and I had left because of the heat and humidity. Ronald was a night owl and could be contacted on any matter at two in the morning, but at ten in the morning he was normally still asleep. He had far better eyesight than I ever did and had studied paleography, so it was natural for me to show him a woodcut with an indistinct artist's name and ask him, with his knowledge of ancient writings, to decipher it. The history of the book was his other professional interest. After my retirement he became a willing collaborator in the bibliographic grubbing needed to organize and write the catalogues of early children's books: *Canadian Children's Books: 1799-1939* and *Books That Shaped Our Mind,* a bibliographical catalogue of selections chiefly from the Arkley Collection of Early and Historical Children's Literature housed in the Special Collections and University Archives Division of the UBC Library.

At the other end of the hall was Professor Anne Piternick, who, among many other things, organized the first National Conference on Canadian Bibliography in 1974. She later participated in the development of an infrastructure program in support of bibliography and archives that was sponsored by the Social Sciences and Humanities Research Council of Canada. She also chaired the first Awards Committee established under the program.

Another colleague at the other end of the hall was Lois M. Bewley, our public library expert. She was nationally recognized for her defence of intellectual freedom and for her strong advocacy of free public library service in Canada and the legislation that made it possible, the First Public Library Act. Free library service has been constantly threatened, as has free access to public parks across Canada. In spite of her many serious undertakings, Professor Bewley has always had a wonderful wit and sense of humour. From all her travels to conferences and library-related events over a period of years, she has amassed an impressively large souvenir button collection.

The library school operated upon Dr. Rothstein's basic philosophy of education, which meant that as faculty members we were to be available for the students eight hours a day every weekday. He felt that teaching went on as much in our offices and in the halls as in the classrooms. This is why, although we had many special lecturers, he was never really enthusiastic about hiring part-time faculty. As director of the School of Librarianship for ten years, Dr. Rothstein was an outstanding administrator and favoured an informal, collegial spirit between professors and students. He used to say, "In seven-and-a-half months, they may well be our colleagues and should be treated as such now."

Shortly after joining the library school faculty, I began my professional writing career with a flourish when, in the winter of 1964, I was asked by an informal committee, the Children's Recreational Reading Council of Ontario, to write a study of Canadian children's books as a 1967 Centennial project. It was published by Oxford

University Press, (Canada) as *The Republic of Childhood*: *A Critical Guide to Canadian Children's Literature in English*. I was fortunate to have an editor and a publisher already in place, since William Toye was a member of the committee. Toye began his career in publishing with Oxford and remained with them until his retirement in 1991. Well-known and respected by Canadian authors and publishers, Toye is widely travelled and regarded as an expert on Canadian history and literature. Now doing freelance work for Oxford, he has always been a meticulous editor and deeply involved with each project he works on, anxious that it be of the highest quality. We worked together on all three editions of *The Republic of Childhood*, and based upon my personal experience, I consider him to be one of Canada's great editors.

Although I felt at home with the literature of my own country, as a child I read randomly, without thinking about patterns or considering aspects such as chronology or region. I organized *The Republic of Childhood* as I organized my courses—by revealing the pattern of literature itself by following the chronology of its development. I was flattered to be asked to take on this project, but in the writing of it I learned much more than the people who had commissioned me could ever have imagined. As a result of my research, I concluded that children's literature could and should be a disciplined critical study. On a visit to Japan I was asked by a Japanese student, rather crossly, how I had the nerve to be a critic of children's literature. I responded quickly and simply by saying that I was in a position to be a critic because I had studied literature in a disciplined way, from the past to the present and through all its changes and innovations, difficulties and triumphs.

The organizational premise of the first edition of *The Republic of Childhood* was to describe the books by genre, which also allowed me to discover what was lacking in our modern literature for the young. I began by writing the historical fiction chapter, and Dr. Rothstein encouraged me to send it to *Canadian Literature*, a journal published at UBC. This proved to be greatly beneficial, as it developed an early interest in the project. As I continued my research, three obvious gaps in our children's literature became apparent: the lack of picturebooks with a Canadian ambience; the lack of a reflection of our multicultural society; and the lack of novels with an urban setting. After all, 94 percent of our urban and multicultural population lives along our border with the United States, and the rest of the country is almost as unpopulated as it was a hundred and fifty years ago. As a consequence, in the 1960s or earlier, a Canadian child could come home from school and say that George Washington was the father of her country. She probably had seen or read about George Washington, Abraham Lincoln and many other famous Americans in any of the D'Aulaires' many illustrated books of American history. In fact, during the first half of the twentieth century, Canadian children were brought up on British and American picturebooks. Had they ever had an opportunity to read a picturebook about the first prime minister of Canada? Not likely.

Only later did I discover in Special Collections at UBC one of Canada's earliest picturebooks. Although Amelia Frances Howard-Gibbons's *An Illustrated Comic Alphabet* is considered our earliest picturebook, dating back to 1859 but not published until 1966 by Oxford University Press, *A Canadian Child's ABC*, written by R.K. Gordon, an English professor at the University of Alberta, and illustrated by Thoreau Macdonald, appeared in 1931. It had something for adults as well as children, the current trend in many contemporary alphabet books. For example, in Gordon's book, "O is for Ottawa":

> To Ottawa from coast to coast
> The chosen come to make the laws.
> For weeks they talk about a lot
> Of different things with scarce a pause:
> The railway line to Hudson Bay,
> Taxes and tariff, immigration,

The great St. Lawrence waterway,

And whether we are yet a nation.

Happily he did not succumb to the usual "A is for aardvark" and "Z is for zebra." Although lacking artistic flair, the realistic pen-and-ink drawings provided children with scenes that were authentically Canadian.

I began *The Republic of Childhood,* as all literature begins, with the myths and legends of our indigenous cultures, our First Nations legends. The 1960s brought a group of non-First Nations retellers to the forefront of our children's books: Frances Fraser of the prairies, Dorothy Reid of Ontario, Kay Hill of eastern Canada and Robert Ayre and Christie Harris of British Columbia. The First Nations legends matched the patterns of legends of other cultures in their evolution but had their own cultural colouration. They had the same simplicity of plot, clarity of style, universality of themes, sparseness of language and awareness of the complexity of human nature in an individual. Human behaviour, evident in its everyday pursuits, does not vary that much over time or across cultures.

Making the First Nations legends accessible to children without oversimplifying them was one of Christie Harris's great contributions. In *Once Upon a Totem*, Harris turned the legends into small stories and personalized the characters, thus making the stories richer in a literary sense than the original legends. The moral intent of each story was always apparent but had a comforting connection to a living child, First Nations or non-First Nations. For example, the famous BC First Nations legend "The Mountain Goats of Temlaham" begins with a child:

Long, long ago there lived an Indian boy, Du'as, who
found one northern summer almost endless. It seemed to
him that the golden tints of autumn would never brighten
the aspen trees along the lower slopes of Stek-yaw-den.

Christie Harris never sacrificed authenticity to modernity. At first I admit to having been uncomfortable with her approach, but the more I read, the more I appreciated what she had accomplished. The stories in *Once Upon a Totem* are based on ethnological reports and on the author's first-hand knowledge. I think the most important contribution that Christie Harris made to our store of First Nations legends arose from the fact that she was in constant communication and consultation with First Nations people. When the cultural appropriation controversy arose in the 1980s, debating whether the First Nations legends should be written or retold by non-First Nations people, Christie Harris escaped criticism because she was at one with her material and always demonstrated her respect for the tellers of the original tales. In addition to acknowledging her as a national treasure for her writing, I always admired Christie Harris for her genuine warmth and unique style of dress. She was a tall, slender woman who always dressed simply but elegantly. She could put on a scarf and look as though she had just stepped out of a Paris salon.

Her later realistic novel, *You Have to Draw the Line Somewhere*, based upon her oldest daughter Moira's experiences, was unusual for the time because it showed an ordinary Canadian family in an interesting situation with convincingly normal child characters. At that time it was also one of the few or only stories about conventional Canadian urban life. I decided to send the book to the newly appointed director of the library school, Roy Stokes, who was on his way to BC with his wife and two young daughters. Upon his arrival he told me that his daughters had been so delighted with the book that it helped reconcile them to leaving their home in England.

When *Son of Raven, Son of Deer: Fables of the Tse-shaht People*, written by the First Nations chief George Clutesi, appeared in 1967, teachers eager to introduce First Nations legends to their students were delighted. Here was a skillfully written collection of stories, easy to follow and filled with humour that children could understand and enjoy. His book was quickly incorporated into the elementary school curriculum. Clutesi was the first First Nations writer to make a breakthrough and write legends that had an appealing universality. Each story was an Aesop-like fable in the standard tradition of folklore dealing with the difference between wisdom and foolishness. In a sense they are highly moral and were used by the First Nations people as a means of teaching the younger generation the difference between right and wrong. I was disappointed that I had to wait until the second edition of *The Republic* to celebrate Clutesi's writing and contribution, because the first edition was published shortly before his book appeared.

Clutesi was an accomplished narrator and told his stories in a direct, engaging manner that I was convinced would be perfect for storytelling and would appeal to children of other cultures. Unfortunately, in this instance I was proved wrong. I had persuaded my volunteer puppet group to perform two stories based on the Clutesi tales, but the children received the presentations with either puzzlement or indifference. Two or three times we rewrote the puppet scripts to make them more accessible to the non-First Nations child. Also, to illustrate the difference between stories from different cultures, the students had designed a new version of "The Three Little Pigs." The three little pigs in their puppet suits were portrayed as little girls, complete with pink ribbons, and stole the show. The experience taught me a lot about cultural dissimilarities in storytelling. The story of the three little pigs was familiar to the children as it has had hundreds of years of retellings and picturebook illustrations shaping it. Also, parents and teachers likely have dramatized it as they tell the story: "I'll huff and I'll puff and I'll blow your house down!" For some reason, the puppetry versions of the Clutesi stories failed to engage their young audiences in a similar fashion.

When working with children, I often was reminded that we can easily make incorrect assumptions about what may appeal to them.

We also must be careful not to underestimate children. Once, I was preparing to tell the story of "The Old Woman and Her Pig" to children in a Burnaby library. Alarmed by how young the children were, I panicked and broke my own "golden rule" by changing the word "sixpence" to "ten cents." As I continued, I felt a little tug on my skirt and a small boy said, "In Burnaby, we say sixpence." As I used to tell my library students, no matter how the situation may change, always stick to your original plan.

First Nations legends lack the pattern of repetition and cumulative effect of many European tales, such as the Steele retelling of "Mr. Fox": "Be bold, be bold, but not too bold, lest that your heart's blood should run cold!" They usually do not feature the mnemonic devices, accumulation and strong, rewarding climax that so often characterize a European legend. My favourite book as a source for telling First Nations legends to children is Dorothy Reid's *Tales of Nanabozho*, chiefly because the stories are short and filled with humour, and are well honed in her retellings. I particularly enjoyed telling "Nanabozho and the Wild Geese," in part because of two little verses that are so easy to remember that children quickly caught on and chanted them along with me. When Nanabozho is boasting, he sings, "Flocks of wild geese up in the sky, Nanabozho flew as far and as high." His boasting is followed by his downfall as the other First Nations people chant:

> High in the autumn sky
> Wild geese are calling.
> Down from the autumn sky
> Nana is falling.

The story is a perfect example of the First Nations trickster legend because the trickster, as always, becomes the butt of the joke. I told this legend at a storytelling festival in Seattle in the 1980s, a period when many of the First Nations peoples were objecting to their stories being told or written by non-First Nations people. I have always been troubled by this attitude. I feel that myth, legend and folklore belong to all peoples. Can only a Greek retell Greek myths? At this particular conference, I happened to be the next speaker after an American First Nations woman who was adamantly opposed to the non-First Nations incursion into their literature. Not intending any disrespect, I stood up and told the Nanabozho story that I had prepared and planned to tell. Fortunately, perhaps because of the humour in the story, no one appeared to take exception to my telling the story. Who can resist laughing at Nanabozho?

The rest of *The Republic of Childhood* fell into established literary compartments. One of the longest chapters was devoted to Canadian historical fiction, even though I found much of the writing uninspired due to the failure of the authors to transcend the events being related. Admittedly, Canadian history is not easy to dramatize. It lacks mythological figures and events, dynamic personalities and eccentrics. Our history does not have the Wars of the Roses, the little princes in the Tower, King Knut ordering the waves back, or King Arthur burning the cakes. Our few great stories of conflict and tension are seldom recorded in books for children. However, in my review of historical fiction published before 1967, I found two outstanding novels that I felt reached beyond the history itself to give the facts universality: *The Whale People* by Roderick Haig-Brown and *Nkwala* by Edith L. Sharp. *The Whale People* has a simple strength and dignity and fittingly reflects the qualities of the people of the Hotsath tribe, "the whale people," living on the west coast of Vancouver Island. Sharp's *Nkwala* is a gentler, quieter story that moves to a swift and dramatic climax as Nkwala risks his life to avoid a battle between his Spokan tribe and the Okanagan tribe. Both stories are successful due to the short time span they cover, their young protagonists and the solid research and skillful writing of the authors. Unfortunately, many early Canadian historical novels are too long on history, too short on fiction, span too broad a time period and lack youthful characters. In the sixties, Canada lacked writers with the skill of Britain's Rosemary Sutcliff, whose historical novels such as

Eagle of the Ninth perfectly meld and balance story and history.

What Canada did have were the perilous adventures of the explorers who opened up our vast country. A biography I feel remains unmatched in Canadian children's literature for its excitement and vitality is *Franklin of the Arctic* by J.S. Lambert, published in 1949. Respectful of the degree of invention that is acceptable when writing an historical narrative, Lambert exhibits great skill in his selection of the available evidence as he describes Franklin's last voyage and ill-fated attempt to find the long-dreamed-of Northwest Passage. Another fine example of a Canadian historical book that is scrupulously faithful to the verifiable facts is Pierre Berton's *The Golden Trail: The Story of the Klondike Gold Rush*, published in 1954. Even the conversations that occur throughout the book were reproduced from personal interviews by Berton or found in diaries and published reports. This memorable account of unbelievable hardships has great appeal for young people. Berton's *The Golden Trail* is likely the best book in our first major Canadian-history series, The Great Stories of Canada, which encompassed more than thirty volumes. On the whole, these were fictionalized accounts of Canadian history and biographies of its important people. The series became quite popular; I even heard of children spending their allowances on the next Great Story of Canada. Many of the stories describe the drive to western Canada, explorers, First Nations people, settlements and the huge fur-trading companies such as the Hudson's Bay Company and the North West Company. As with most series, some books were considerably better than others. I am sure I read all of them, but found a number of them rather tedious and soon found myself reaching for a British mystery.

In addition to Berton's description of the first Canadian gold rush, I remember most vividly and with pleasure Roderick Haig-Brown's *Captain of the Discovery*, chronicling George Vancouver's time on the West Coast. Haig-Brown was already recognized as a writer for children and managed to keep a satisfying balance between history and fiction. Many of the Canadian offerings in history and biography written for a young audience also failed to engage me sufficiently to keep me awake nights. Almost in desperation, and recalling my childhood reading of Seton and Roberts, I devoted a chapter in *The Republic* to the realistic animal story, a genre which has almost disappeared in these modern times and been replaced by many of the new information books and series on animals and wildlife.

Up to the sixties, books of poetry and verse were so scarce and eclectic, so imitative of Robert Louis Stevenson and A.A. Milne, that they were not worth including in the book. Baby books were simply non-existent. Canadian babies certainly did not have a waterproof book to throw into the bath water. Canada also lacked a literary environment that would nurture the writing of fantasy. As a young country, it did not have the oral stories and traditions that had become an integral aspect of older, more-established countries. However, a Canadian setting did inspire a few books of fantasy written in the early part of the twentieth century, mostly by American writers.

In 1950, Catherine Anthony Clark, with her book *The Golden Pine Cone*, became Canada's first fantasy writer of note. The mountains and lakes of British Columbia became the background for her stories as she drew upon her deep love and knowledge of the Kootenay area of the province. Clark's great strength was her characters; she peopled her books with the familiar figures of First Nations chiefs and princesses and with uniquely created spirit-folk characters such as the Rock Puck, the Ice Folk, the Head Canada Goose and the Lake Snake. Although each of her books had the characteristic plot of a quest story, her approach was always fresh. For example, in *The One-Winged Dragon* she introduces, to my knowledge, the first Chinese characters in Canadian children's fiction. Her children are rather stock characters, always a boy and a girl, always close friends, not completely happy at home, but always independent, unselfish, adventurous and happy with themselves and the settings in which their adventures take place. For these reasons, none of Clark's characters has the depth or sensitivity of the children in books such as Frances H. Burnett's *The Secret Garden*, but her books are enchanting nonetheless.

In my chapter on fantasy, I was not kind in my assessment of Mazo de la Roche's first and only children's book, *The Song of Lambert*. I wrote: "Mazo de la Roche... equated fantasy with fanciful incidents and allegorical names—the butcher is called Mr. Blood and the dyspeptic millionaire is Mr. Van Grunt. The author so fails to arouse any sympathy for Lambert (a lamb, of course) that the reader longs for him to be divested of his human characteristics and converted into chops." Many years later Margaret Laurence quoted me in her autobiography, but she did not reveal any resentment: "in 1970 I wrote a fantasy called *Jason's Quest*, and Sheila Egoff said it was the worst animal fantasy that she had ever read." Then Laurence simply continued on with her own life story. I found this gracious on the part of such a famous author. Many friends of writers whom I criticized have not hesitated to communicate their displeasure to me.

A discussion of folk and fairy tales ended the chapter on fantasy. Folktales are by definition the product of non-literate societies, but a number of Canadian writers adapted and recreated the folktales that had originated in their European, Asian or African heritages. *The Golden Phoenix and other French-Canadian Fairy Tales* contains eight French-Canadian folktales collected by Marius Barbeau, a noted ethnologist and anthropologist, and retold by Michael Hornyansky, who gave them a polished modern treatment, creating what I would describe as literary fairy tales. These stories had been brought to Canada by the French colonists three hundred years earlier. Before 1967, *The Golden Phoenix* collection was the best example we had of foreign folklore that could also be regarded as indigenous and part of Canadian literature.

I called the final chapter in *The Republic of Childhood* "And All the Rest: Stories" to encompass the books that were too few or diverse to warrant a separate grouping. This section gave me the opportunity to discuss the Canadian theme of conflict against the wilderness. I believe that no branch of Canadian children's literature has produced such a uniformly high level of achievement or universality as that found in the tales of outdoor adventure and survival. With their ability to combine narrative skill and dramatic settings with descriptions of human endurance and courage, Roderick Haig-Brown and Farley Mowat excelled in this genre far beyond all others, both in Canada and worldwide. With the appearance of *Lost in the Barrens*, Farley Mowat became almost instantly famous as a writer for children, and many successes followed, including *The Black Joke*, a lively modern pirate story set in and around Newfoundland. In fact, he became so popular that in my day he was referred to as "Mr. Canada." When a teenager, my oldest nephew, to whom I used to feed books, said to me indignantly, "You never told me about Farley Mowat!" Mowat became a kind of touchstone for quality in books for children. I wanted every Canadian child to know *Owls in the Family*. Nowadays Wol, the extrovert owl, and Weep, the introvert, likely would have their own television program. Based on my reading of Seton and Roberts, I never felt for a moment that Mowat's *Never Cry Wolf* was anything but accurate in its study of the family life of wolves.

The first edition of *The Republic of Childhood* in 1967 turned out to be a modest publishing success, perhaps because it was the first of its kind and perhaps because, rather than merely describing the literature, I had organized it and given it shape. Another difference between *The Republic* and critical guides from other countries is that I often highlighted the strengths of specific books and authors by identifying the weaknesses of books in a comparable genre. My hope and intention were that my comments would prove to be of value to other Canadian writers. Also, in order to create a full-length book, I felt I had no recourse but to comment on some of our poorer material as well as showcasing our best, even at the risk of offending some authors. At that time Canada did not have a rich, substantial body of literature for children as we had only a few outstanding books in print that were nationally recognized, such as *Anne of Green Gables* and perhaps a few works by Farley Mowat.

Shortly after the publication of *The Republic of Childhood* in 1967, I teamed with university colleagues Gordon Stubbs and Leslie Ashley to compile a selection of critical articles and essays on children's literature. The result was published by Oxford (Canada) in 1969 as *Only Connect: Readings on Children's Literature*, with a partially revised edition published in 1980. In the early 1990s, rapid social changes and the escalating quantity of books for young people convinced the three of us that there was sufficient material of quality to warrant a completely new collection. We invited a university colleague, Wendy Sutton, my co-author on this book, to join our team, and the four of us found and read hundreds of critical articles, primarily from periodicals, and sometimes newspapers, looking for selections that we felt offered important insights and informed contemporary thinking. As with the two previous editions of *Only Connect*, our primary aim was to find selections that were fresh and illuminating and dealt with children's literature as an essential part of the whole realm of literary activity. Reluctant to give up a number of stimulating and rather controversial commentaries on such topics as the impact of political correctness and the increase of adult social and political issues prevalent in books for the young, we included several in order to spark interest and debate on some of the issues related to literature for young readers. The third edition of *Only Connect: Readings on Children's Literature*, with a completely new selection of more than forty essays, was published in 1996, again by Oxford University Press.

In the late 1960s I was asked to make a submission on Canadian children's books to the Royal Commission on Book Publishing which was finally published in 1972. The report was a major effort, but the results of my study assessing the state of publishing in Canada were distressingly negative. It was a study in considerable depth, as I had sent questionnaires to most of the major publishers at that time. The majority of the replies that I received were filled with expressions of gloom and doom. It became apparent that in a country with the second-largest landmass in the world and a relatively small population, smaller, in fact, than the population of California, an influx of government money for publishing was crucial. Many other countries with small populations were taking active measures to preserve their culture. At that time Denmark, for example, deposited a copy of each new Danish children's book into every school and public library in the country. Understandably, this was not the practice in countries with large populations such as Great Britain and the United States. Canada also was hampered by its pervasive regionalism. In the United States, a book set in New York City can sell anywhere, as it would if set in London, but this was not the situation in Canada. I had already discovered in writing the first edition of *The Republic of Childhood* that children in western Canada had never heard of or read New Brunswick's Charles G.D. Roberts, and children in eastern Canada had never heard of or read Vancouver Island's Roderick Haig-Brown. Although these two authors are not likely to be familiar to Canadian children today, I am confident that young people in the twenty-first century, through the assistance of dedicated teachers and librarians, are familiar with books by writers from all across Canada.

The main thesis of my submission to the Royal Commission was that we needed Canadian experiences to be featured in the books written for our young readers. No imported literature can or will tell children about their own country. Our children's books, more than books for adults, should show what Canada and Canadians are like, what values we respect, and how we view our present and our future. Just as Charles Dickens's novels tell us much about Victorian England, children's books in Canada need to reflect the characteristics of our own society. It may be a reflection in miniature, but it will be accurate and emotionally valuable. Many Canadian children's books, even those that are otherwise rather mediocre, have been informed by a deeply felt response to the land and to its history. In this respect, our writers have used the Canadian experience successfully, but at a cost. By concentrating on the land itself, Canadian writers for many years tended to slight other aspects of our country such as urban life and the mélange of ethnic backgrounds of our citizenry.

CHAPTER FIVE

As Happy as Kings

*I*n 1968, nearly two decades after the fantasies of Catherine Anthony Clark were published, a new wave of original modern fantasies emerged in which fantasy intruded on the reality of a specific and recognizable urban Canadian setting. In Janet Lunn's first fantasy, *Double Spell* (*Twin Spell* in the United States), twin sisters are strangely compelled to buy a valuable old doll from an antique shop. The doll intrudes upon and changes their lives. In earlier fantasies such as *Alice's Adventures in Wonderland* and C.S. Lewis's *The Chronicles of Narnia*, the protagonists move into a fantasy world. In other books such as J.R.R. Tolkien's *The Hobbit* and *The Lord of the Rings*, the fictional characters are situated in a fantasy world to begin with. But in Lunn's *Double Spell*, the supernatural world breaks into the real world. There is no separation between the two. And in reading fantasy, you must either accept it in its entirety or reject it. You must wholeheartedly exercise Samuel Coleridge's "willing suspension of disbelief." I swallowed all of Lunn's world, characters, situation and setting. Other fantasies in a Canadian context, such as those by Catherine Anthony Clark, use broadly drawn

1. Sheila's family home in Galt, Ontario, 110 Wellington Street (left side).

2. Sheila's mother, Lucy Joyce Egoff, 1891-1948.

3. Lillian Smith, 1887–1983.

4. Fairy Tale Room, Boys and Girls House, ca. 1928.

5. Boys and Girls House, Toronto Public Library, ca. 1922.

6. With the family dog, Aussie, in her brother George's backyard.

7. Enjoying some summer sun.

8. Dining out in New York with her cousin James before sailing to London, 1947.

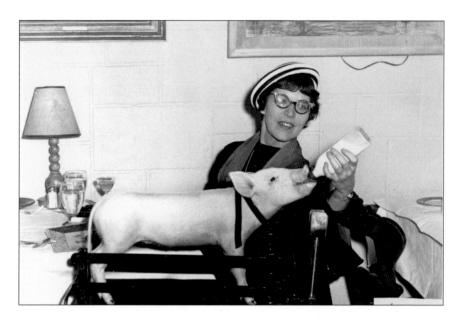

9. A free Montreal moment while organizing the 1960 ALA/CLA conference.

10. Aerial view of Main Library, UBC, ca. 1960.

11. Faculty members in the Faculty Lounge, UBC, 1962
— l. to r. Ronald Hagler, Sheila Egoff, Sam Rothstein.

12. Talking to Sam Rothstein, 1963.

13. Wearing one of her many pairs of fashionable glasses, 1966.

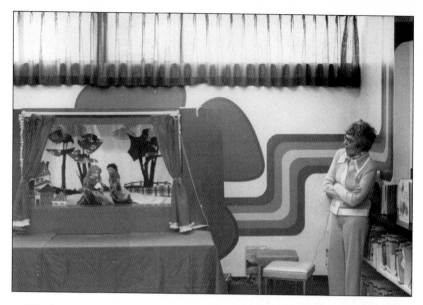

14. Watching a puppet show at the Burnaby Public Library, ca. 1973.

15. With Stanley and Rose Arkley, ca. 1976.

16. Welcoming the world to the first Pacific Rim Conference on Children's Literature, 1976.

17. Dancing joyfully at her eightieth birthday party, 1998.

18. SLAIS 25TH anniversary celebration
—l. to r. Sheila, Lois Bewley, Judi Saltman, Basil Stuart-Stubbs, Anne Piternick.

19. With author Kit Pearson, a former student and close friend.

20. Celebrating the nominees for the Sheila A. Egoff Children's Literature Prize.

Writers of fantasy join all other fine writers of the past in taking childhood seriously which, in turn, allowed them to write with some playfulness, an uncondescending playfulness, for they wrote from the child that lingered within themselves. … Still, for the older fantasists, for the subcreators of magical otherwheres, these journeys were not undertaken to escape reality, but to illuminate it, to transport us to worlds different from the real world, while demonstrating certain immutable truths that persist in any and every possible world, real and imaginary. —Thursday's Child

landscapes as backgrounds. Janet Lunn provides named streets, specific little shops and the familiar lakeshore waterfront of Toronto. It was heady stuff.

Soon after the publication of *Double Spell*, Ruth Nichols appeared with *A Walk out of the World* and *The Marrow of the World*. Nichols's children's fantasy could stand proudly beside that of Lewis and Tolkien. Where Catherine Anthony Clark's children stepped only lightly into something fantastic, Nichols's children were driven into a fantasy world by some form of unhappiness. At that time, this was stern stuff in a Canadian novel for children. Nichols believed in Tolkien's theory of fantasy: that you leave this world and enter another or secondary world to be healed of what is ailing you in the real world. Tolkien considered the secondary world to be as important as our primary world. Nichols also believed in this form of classic, high fantasy: the great struggle between good and evil. Her children take on challenges in a kind of epic struggle, both for themselves and for the larger consequences involved. Nichols also did Canadian fantasy a favour by placing her stories in recognizable environments such as Vancouver in British Columbia and Georgian Bay in Ontario. Just consider British fantasy, where lanes, hills and rivers have been named for centuries, whereas usually in their reading our children have had to move through great anonymous Canadian landscapes.

In 1970, when the School of Librarianship's BLS program was extended to become a two-year MLS program, I was able to introduce a course devoted to literature for young adults. YA publications seemed to be taking over, in large part because publishers had begun labelling books written for readers as young as ten as "young adult." The literary world was being flooded with such books and I felt that I should address the phenomenon with my library students. Little did I know what I was getting myself into. First, I had to give myself a course in current young adult fiction. When I was a young reader, I had moved directly from childhood reading to adult reading, from *The Secret Garden* to *Anna Karenina*, as did most people my age. I remember an extensive young adult collection at the Toronto Public Library, where the shelves were filled with adult books that would be of special interest to the teenaged reader. Consequently, I began by modeling my young adult course on the TPL's collection by choosing adult books I felt young people between fifteen and nineteen years old would enjoy. Among others, I selected Emily Brontë's *Wuthering Heights*, Jane Austen's *Pride and Prejudice*, Fyodor Dostoevsky's *Crime and Punishment* and D.H. Lawrence's *Sons and Lovers*. I also looked for Canadian adult books that could be used in the same way, but that proved to be much more difficult. Two that I recall including were *Maria Chapdelaine* by Louis Hémon and *As for Me and My House* by Sinclair Ross.

I also began reading and using some widely read American young adult "problem novels" such as J.D. Salinger's *The Catcher in the Rye*, S.E. Hinton's *The Outsiders* and Paul Zindel's *The Pigman*. To my surprise I found myself in a whole new world of teenage angst with its self-centred, first-person narratives and themes of alienation, hostility and search for identity, and topics such as gangs, drugs, alcoholism and abortion. When I started bemoaning the lack of intensity of emotion and literary quality in these "new realism" books, my library students, most of whom were from the prairie provinces, told me that such books were all that had been available in their community libraries. According to them, during their teens they had been introduced to little other than the American "problem novel," which had begun to be prevalent in the mid-sixties. I was aware that to give young people the best is difficult, but I had not realized the extent to which people in the book world were apparently content to give youth books that, on the whole, were shallow and mediocre. As Lillian Smith wrote in *The Unreluctant Years*, "To tolerate the mediocre and the commonplace is to misunderstand the purpose of book selection and the significance of literature."

In my eclectic reading when I was young, I had come across H.G. Wells's *The War of the Worlds* and Jules Verne's *Twenty Thousand Leagues under the Sea*, although at the time I did not know the term science fiction. For me, they were just great stories. However, when teaching the young adult literature course, I realized that I had to deal with what was now known as science fiction. I prepared very carefully. I thought the lecture had gone well until one of the students in the class came up to me and told me that it had been the worst lecture he had ever heard. "You don't seem to know a thing about science fiction," he said. So I said, "I will give you preparation time to prepare the next lecture for the class," to which he agreed. As I sat in the classroom listening to him, I realized that we had two completely different perspectives. He was discussing science fiction as an aficionado, whereas I was viewing it from my usual critical stance as a librarian considering what merited purchase for the library. However, as a result of his presentation, I developed a greater understanding of science fiction and read as widely as I could in the genre.

I taught the young adult course until I retired in 1983 and, over the years, saw our relatively few Canadian authors of fiction for adolescents skillfully avoid the overly simplistic content and the

Children may not always be able to judge and appreciate
excellence in writing, but this fact, far from permitting
inferior work, places on writers the obligation to meet
the highest standards of integrity and artistry.

—Only Connect:
Readings on Children's Literature (1969)

shallowness of the American problem novel. As a genre, young adult
realistic fiction hardly existed in Canada until the 1980s, but I did find
Kevin Major's *Hold Fast*, Elizabeth Brochmann's *What's the Matter,*
Girl?, Brian Doyle's *Up to Low* and Beatrice Culleton's *In Search of*
April Raintree to be novels that offer authentic patterns of behaviour,
depth of characterization, and sharp insights into life that are worthy
of their teenage readers.

When preparing my lectures, I had noticed that beautifully illustrated editions of individual European folktales were receiving positive reviews. I was surprised that Canadian publishers had not taken
more initiative to produce picturebooks depicting local backgrounds
or featuring some of the fascinating material available in the national
archives in Ottawa. Feeling that Canada was once again falling behind
the United States and Europe, I suggested to Bill Toye, chief editor of
Oxford University Press (Canada), that he publish an illustrated version of a single First Nations legend. He agreed and said that he had
the perfect illustrator in mind: Elizabeth Cleaver, a young Montreal
artist. The collaboration between Toye as editor and reteller and
Cleaver as illustrator resulted in *The Mountain Goats of Temlaham*, a
BC legend, and *How Summer Came to Canada*, set in New Brunswick.
Cleaver's creative use of collage, paper-tearing and real objects such
as cedar boughs resulted in picturebooks that are visually striking and
that continue to be prized by schools and libraries.

In 1972, because an English-speaking judge was needed, the CLA chose to send me to Portugal to sit on the Hans Christian Andersen Jury. Established in 1956, the Andersen Awards were the first international book awards to be given to an author or illustrator who has made an outstanding contribution to children's literature. Because I thought they were so innovative and special, I took several copies each of Elizabeth Cleaver's two illustrated First Nations stories on the presumption that I would have a chance to exhibit them. I surprised myself by giving a full-blown speech in which I described the collage-illustrated interpretations of these two famous legends and explained their value and contribution to our Canadian culture. To my great delight, and in spite of the fact that Canada was not a member of the International Board on Books for Young People (IBBY), Cleaver was voted onto the Honour List for illustration. I was thrilled that these important books were praised on the international stage, but sadly disappointed that recognition in Canada was not forthcoming. In each of the children's libraries in Europe that I visited following the conference, I found announcements of the winners of the Andersen Awards. I had telegraphed the CLA to inform them of the recognition given to Cleaver and Canada, but to my knowledge no public announcement of her award was ever made. I am gratified to report that Canada is now a full-fledged member of IBBY and has the official right to make Canadian nominations for the Hans Christian Andersen Award.

Because the first edition of *The Republic of Childhood* was out of print, Oxford University Press suggested in the early seventies that I work on a second edition, which was published in 1975. When contemplating the work of the second edition, I felt that I had discovered a flaw in our earlier critiques of First Nations material. In Canada, even though the quantity of aboriginal material had increased, we had lumped it all under one catch-all phrase—Indian legends. In the second edition, the First Nations legend material was expanded to include Inuit legends, stories primarily filled with a fear of the environment. Roland Melzack's *The Day Tuk Became a Hunter & Other Eskimo Stories* was the book that made me realize how different these stories are from other First Nations legends. The Inuit stories depict a people who were more violent, vengeful and stoical than their southern counterparts. Melzack's book appears to be the first Canadian collection of its kind for children. Earlier American collections of First Nations material often turned the severely realistic stories into gentle animal fantasies. For authenticity, Canadian authors had to rely upon Knud Rasmussen and Vilhjalmur Stefansson, researchers who recorded the stories just as they had heard them, without any literary intervention. The following was told by Inuit Aua to Rasmussen, the Danish explorer and ethnologist, in 1921:

> We fear the weather spirit of earth, that
>   we must fight against to wrest our food
>   from land and sea. We fear Sila.
> We fear death and hunger in the cold
>   snow huts.
> We fear Takanakapsaluk, the great woman
>   who down at the bottom of the sea
>   rules over all the beasts of the sea.
> We fear the sickness that we meet with daily
>   all around us; not death, but the suffering.
> We fear the evil spirits of life, those of the air,
>   of the sea and earth, that can help wicked
>   shamans to harm their fellow man.
> We fear the souls of dead human beings
>   and of the animals we have killed.

For many years the pool of our Inuit legends has lain dormant in anthropological studies and archival collections. The Inuit artists and sculptors, not the writers, have claimed the attention and acclaim of

It appears that current children's books reflect the society they were written in to a degree not known since the seventeenth century and that they are overwhelmingly carrying on the traditional mission of children's books: to inform and instruct the young. There have been changes in style and theme in the books published in the last few years, and it is not surprising that the greatest changes appear in American fiction. Even a superficial study of North American society in the sixties reveals confusion, uneasiness, a shifting of values, a preoccupation with the psychology of individual and group problems, and a strong desire, particularly on the part of young people, to be told the truth, no matter how it distresses adults to tell it to them. —Only Connect: Readings on Children's Literature (1969)

people interested in the culture of the North. However, we know that storytelling went on during the long Arctic nights and that, among their people, the Inuit storytellers achieved the status of the bards and troubadours of early European culture. The Inuit themselves most valued oral literature. Inuit legends are a perfect example of how stories reflect cultures; most of their stories describe hunting, whether for food, fuel, clothing or shelter. This subject matter makes sense when you consider that there is scarcely any region on earth that presents conditions more severe and challenging to human existence than the High Arctic.

While working on the second edition of *The Republic of Childhood*, I found two more stars to praise—Ann Blades and Dennis Lee. In 1971, the British Columbia illustrator and storyteller Ann Blades arrived on the picture-storybook scene with a book that is still popular, *Mary of Mile 18*. Blades had taught for many years in the northern part of the province, and her knowledge and understanding of the young, as well as her artistic skill, shine from every one of her books. *Mary of Mile 18* tells the story of a little Mennonite girl living at Mile 18 in northern British Columbia. She wants to keep a young wolf pup as a pet, but her father, driven by his survival mentality as a farmer, orders her to take it to the woods, saying, "Our animals must work for us or give us food." Happily, as is the case in a great majority of children's books, the ending provides safety and security for Mary and her wolf pup. *Mary of Mile 18* is one of the few Canadian books, like *Sajo and her Beaver People*, that depicts an emotional bond between humans and animals.

The other star was versifier Dennis Lee, author of *Alligator Pie*, *Nicholas Knock* and others. Never before or since have I known a Canadian children's book to become so immediately and justifiably popular. Dennis Lee's appeal for children lies in his strong rhyming schemes, which children discovered easily worked into chants. Along with his chants and his Canadian references, which are catchy and unusual, there was "A Song for Ookpik," which established that he could write poetry as well as verse.

> Ookpik, Ookpik Dance with Us,
> Till our Lives Go Luminous…
>
> Ookpik, Ookpik By your Grace,
> Help us Live in Our own Space.

Dennis Lee became the Father Goose for Canadian children, bringing images of Canada and a sense of fun into the lives of young children.

Another important new illustrator on the picture-storybook scene was William Kurelek, discovered by May Cutler of Tundra Books. I found his books a little disappointing because written commentaries

Children also need time to become intimate with a small number of picture books, to form friendships with favourite characters as they do with their own families and peers. It is this intimacy that forms a child's stepping-stone to future worthwhile literary and artistic experiences. —Thursday's Child

rather than sequential narrative episodes accompany his paintings. I understood the art well enough as paintings, but not as illustrations intended to enhance a story. While his books are always authentic and informative, the paintings parallel rather than extend the text.

My early childhood reading had told me much about the Ukrainians in Manitoba, but I was astonished to read about prairie people working in a lumber camp. However, when Kurelek's *Lumberjack* appeared in 1974, I knew that its portrayal would be authentic. Shortly after the book was published, I was in a rather modest restaurant in Vancouver. On reading the menu, beginning with the appetizers, I came across the entry "Caviar—$50 per person." Amazed, I asked the waitress, "Who in the world can afford fifty dollars for just one serving?" to which she replied, "The men who come in from the lumber camps." Having learned from Kurelek of the hardships and dangers such workers faced, I sincerely hoped that they enjoyed their treat.

Both Ann Blades and William Kurelek were writers and illustrators of picture-storybooks rather than creators of picturebooks. To me a picturebook is a literary work in which the illustrations and text are interdependent. Picturebooks have a fluidity that is lacking in the more formal layout of the picture-storybook. The picturebook as a genre came late in the development of Canadian children's literature and exploded into our bookstores and libraries almost simultaneously with the explosion, in 1976, of children's contemporary novels. Suddenly picturebooks became the most lucrative part of the Canadian children's book publishing industry as publishers were shrewd enough to capitalize on the financial advantages of co-publishing with other national and international publishers. By the 1980s a plethora of picturebooks was being published in this country. Many of these picturebooks were readily exportable and many do not have a Canadian setting but are written, illustrated and published by Canadians and deserving of attention.

I well remember finishing what I considered to be the last line of the revised *The Republic of Childhood* and putting my head down on top of my typewriter and weeping. I felt that there had been no appreciable change in Canadian children's literature since 1967, whereas the British and especially the Americans were speeding ahead with important insights into the lives of modern children and young adults. I concluded that the problem with Canadian children's books was the banality of the writing and the predictable fictional situations that many Canadian authors created. In the mid-seventies, I saw no future in Canada for literature for young people.

To my great surprise and relief, around 1976, unfortunately after the second edition of *The Republic of Childhood* had been published, Canadian books for young people began to change dramatically, with their themes and situations reflecting contemporary society as never before. It was as if every author, illustrator and particularly publisher had been waiting in the wings to make an appearance. Most exciting! There were now more publishers, more prizes, more media interest, more children reading and certainly more skillful writers. I attribute many of these changes to the rise of small publishers such as Kids Can Press, Tundra Books, Annick Press, The Women's Press, Groundwood Books in 1978, and in the mid-eighties Orca Book Publishers. But perhaps the most meaningful explanation of this very welcome development in publishing for young people was the infusion of government money for publishing and the grants to authors from the Canada Council, initiated in 1957, and provincial arts councils.

Initially the output from these small presses was rather disappointing, with the exception of publications from Tundra Books. In my writing and teaching, I tried to identify the best of these newer Canadian children's books, and I found writers who loved our land and who wanted to be honest with children. However, even though I admired the work of talented writers such as Brian Doyle, Kevin Major, Janet Lunn, Kit Pearson, Monica Hughes and Sarah Ellis, I concluded that, on the whole, Canadian authors for young people were still just too cautious. We did not have equivalents to the boldness or daring of American novels such as Louise Fitzhugh's *Harriet the Spy*, Jean Craighead George's *Julie of the Wolves*, Scott O'Dell's *Island of the Blue Dolphins* or Katherine Paterson's *Bridge to Terabithia*.

In the years between the second edition of *The Republic of Childhood* and the 1990 edition with co-author Judith Saltman, Canadian children's literature changed dramatically, becoming vibrant and vital. Because the 1975 edition did not reflect these significant changes, I considered it a failure. However, just after the second edition was published, something happened involving our literature for young people that cheered me up—the first Pacific Rim Conference on Children's Literature. The conference was the idea of the second director of the library school, Roy Stokes, former head of the Loughborough Library School near London, England. He was a great reader of children's books, in part because he had two daughters with whom to share them. The Loughborough conferences, which Roy initiated, were very loosely organized, but when I heard that the committee was considering Canada for the next conference site, I immediately wrote to offer the library school and Vancouver as its base. When I received the letter of refusal and news that Toronto had been chosen, I staggered into Mr. Stokes's office and practically collapsed. It had never crossed my mind that the people in charge would refuse an offer from their founder. Roy took it very calmly. "Never mind, Sheila," he said, "we'll do our own."

The first Pacific Rim Conference on Children's Literature, held in May 1976, was a huge success, thanks chiefly to my students, the teacher librarians and the library school secretarial staff who oversaw the administration of the event. The planning took two years, and with speakers from ten countries it was the largest international conference on children's literature ever held in Canada. The roster of presenters was the most impressive that could have been assembled at that time. Among the speakers were Leon Garfield and Edward Blishen from England, Ivan Southall from Australia, Momoko Ishii from Japan, Vilasini Perumbulavil from Singapore, Jean Karl from the United States and Elizabeth Cleaver, Ruth Nichols, Suzanne Martel, Claude Aubry and May Cutler from Canada. Although I could not have every Canadian author and illustrator speak, many were invited and had their way paid so that they could mingle with the delegates.

The last day of the conference was devoted entirely to Canadian children's books, which must have been a first in Canada. For the Canadian sessions, the registration rose dramatically, exceeding all expectations. The students came to me saying, "Sheila, we just can't control the numbers. They're coming in the windows and coming in the doors." So I said, "Let them all come in." The registration rose from five hundred to eight hundred for that one day. I had asked the first director of the library school, Dr. Samuel Rothstein, to be chairperson for Canada Day. I have never seen anyone work so hard. He attended the whole conference and looked up all the Canadian books and talked to their authors; his introductions of the authors and publishers deserved to have been recorded. All of those who spoke, whether authors, publishers or editors, were rather pessimistic about the future of Canadian publishing, and most of their concerns had to do with the economics of publishing. I am happy to report that following the first Pacific Rim Conference on Children's Literature, and in particular the success of Canada Day, most conferences in this country now have a large component on Canadian children's books and their creators, often sufficient to fill a number of days.

Although it took me more than a year to edit the papers given at the Pacific Rim Conference, I was determined that those who had attended the conference, as well as those working with children and children's literature, would have access to the insights provided by the impressive spectrum of presenters. *One Ocean Touching: Papers from the first Pacific Rim Conference on Children's Literature* was published in 1979 and offers readers the specialized views of writers, illustrators, retellers, educators, librarians, publishers and editors from nine Pacific Rim countries. For me, this anthology demonstrates that children's literature is undeniably a relevant part of the modern world and encompasses and reflects its delights and successes as well as its problems.

Toward the end of the 1970s, the ALA asked me to write an update of Lillian Smith's *The Unreluctant Years*. Without hesitation, I refused the invitation as I did not believe her book needed to be updated; the criteria she had established for assessing children's literature were still valid. However, I said that if they were interested, I was willing to write my own book in which I would attempt to assess the main trends, features and accomplishments in children's literature over the past quarter of a century. The ALA was most supportive, and *Thursday's Child: Trends and Patterns in Contemporary Children's Literature* was published in 1981. The following year I received the ALA's Ralph Shaw Award for *Thursday's Child*. I was particularly pleased with this honour because it was a recognition by my peers of my scholarship related to children's literature in an international context.

In 1979 I was invited to give the Arbuthnot Lecture at the College of Library Science, University of South Carolina, where I learned a very important lesson. I titled my talk "Beyond the Garden Wall," and in it I criticized without mercy Judy Blume's *Are You There God? It's*

Me, Margaret. My presentation appeared to be well-received. While I was answering questions and accepting congratulations, I noticed a young woman waiting to speak to me. She graciously said how much she had enjoyed my speech, but then went on to tell me that when she was a young teenager, Blume's *Margaret* had meant a great deal to her: "I don't think I would have made it through my teenage years without that book." My lesson: You can never predict the impact a book—even one you dislike—will have on a reader.

Shortly before my retirement, I was pleased to be invited to write an article, "Children's Literature in English," for the 1983 edition of *The Oxford Companion to Canadian Literature.* It was not an easy assignment, because by the 1980s our literature had begun to expand rapidly. How to combine the past and the present with very little space in which to do it? The task was daunting. However, I recalled the advice of Lewis Carroll's Red King to the White Rabbit: "Begin at the beginning and go on till you come to the end: then stop." Fortunately, my very good friend Bill Toye was my editor once again, and I travelled to Toronto to work for several nights on the article with him. For me, no effort has ever been too great if it provides an opportunity to promote Canadian children's literature.

I was surprised and honoured when a number of my former students applied for and received a government grant to put on a one-day conference in 1983 to mark my retirement from the School of Librarianship at UBC. The event was held at a hotel on Denman Street in downtown Vancouver and was attended by friends, colleagues, family, authors, storytellers and former students. The program began with Kit Pearson, Sarah Ellis, Judi Saltman, children's librarian Judi Walker and Janice Douglas, director of Youth Services and Programs for the Vancouver Public Library, presenting readings from some of my favourite books such as *Winnie-the-Pooh* and *Charlotte's Web.* The morning continued with Sam Rothstein wittily recalling "The Sheila Years," and author Suzanne Martel amusing everyone with her wonderful humour. After lunch there were breakout sessions related to children's programs and books. Following a social get-together and dinner, the evening program began with a talk by Claude Aubry, the former chief librarian of the Ottawa Public Library. This was followed by his presenting me with the Claude Aubry Award, a biennial award given to an individual for distinguished service within the field of children's literature. Don Mills then put on a puppet show that was a "take off" of me, much to the obvious recognition and delight of those attending. The evening's program ended with Alice Kane telling one of her classic Irish folktales. To quote an old English folktale, she had a storytelling voice "that would hold children from their play and old men from the chimney corners."

As I think back on that event, I recall the great generosity I experienced from everyone involved. For example, as a surprise for me, those organizing the conference had arranged to have George and Lou Egoff, my brother and sister-in-law from Ontario, attend the function. The whole affair began with a cocktail party held at the UBC Faculty Club the evening preceding the conference. I learned later that George and Lou had arrived two hours early and that the manager had permitted them to order dinner using my faculty club number. I remember this vividly because they had themselves a marvellous lobster dinner while I had had nothing to eat all day before the party! It was certainly a very special day for me, as any difficulties that may have arisen during the conference were kept from me. As far as I knew, everything took place without a hitch. The conference was a most satisfying conclusion to my twenty-one years as a full-time faculty member of the School of Librarianship, newly named the School of Library, Archival and Information Studies in 1984, the year after my retirement.

CHAPTER SIX

Up the Mountain-Sides of Dreams

$\mathcal{T}$he day after I closed the office door on the top floor of the north wing of UBC's Main Library, I moved into my new office in Special Collections and began working full-time on classifying the Arkley Collection of Early and Historical Children's Literature, which had been generously given to the school in 1976 during the Pacific Rim Conference. Housed in the Special Collections and University Archives Division, the Arkley Collection was initially over three thousand volumes, chiefly American and British, but also containing valuable Canadian material. Over the years the collection has been expanded, thanks to generous gifts of books and money.

Rose Arkley had specified in her will that the collection be given to the School of Librarianship because she and her husband were impressed with the children's literature and librarianship work being done at UBC. They felt it far exceeded that being done at any other library school in Canada or the United States. Rose Arkley had been a well-known American primary school teacher, and her husband, Stanley, was a Canadian who had attended UBC. As a member of the UBC graduation class of 1929, and reflecting his interest in early children's books, Stanley arranged for the class reunion gift to the university to be an extensive *Alice's Adventures in Wonderland* collection that includes original editions, different versions, translations and books by and about Lewis Carroll. Stan Arkley was the western American representative for Doubleday Publishers, and he and Rose had lived in Seattle where members of their family still reside and continue their interest in the collection.

I began by plunging into the work of organizing the Arkley Collection and reading the books in order to identify those that were to be included in the catalogue. With the money that accompanied the gift of the Arkley Collection, I began training a research assistant to do the detailed descriptions needed for classifying first editions and early books. The bare-bones descriptions that characterize the Library of Congress system do not include details of the binding, the end papers or the appended advertisements that often help establish a date of publication. In short, the unique qualities of each book are recorded according to rare-book formulae so that there is no doubt which edition is being described. Unfortunately, I was unable to get a grant to continue the work on the Arkley, so in order to obtain one of the planned catalogues of early books underway I began the more manageable task of preparing the material for a catalogue of UBC's smaller collection of early Canadian children's books. I read every one of the approximately eight hundred early Canadian books in Special Collections as I felt it was important to know each book intimately, especially as I then would have to decide which books were to be analyzed, described and annotated.

Although I had a telephone in my little office, I did not have a computer, and each night I would sneak books home so that I could write up my notes on my computer. Monday through Friday, I would catch the bus to UBC to work on the collection, but it proved to be slow work as, initially, I did not have anyone to help me. Fortunately Margaret Burke began working with me on Fridays, and Roy Stokes, a skilled bibliographer, visited me weekly to help solve difficult bibliographical problems that I had identified as requiring his expertise. Establishing the criteria that confirm that a book was written for children proved to be difficult. The typical protagonist of much early North American writing was a male in his late teens or early twenties as the heroes of these early stories had to be old enough to have the skills and resources needed to survive in the wilderness. Nowadays the age of the protagonist is normally closer to the age of the prospective reader. There also were few female protagonists, and the books were less sophisticated than those published for today's children.

I used ninety sources, such as publishers' records and publications by the British Museum and the National Library of Canada, to authenticate the bibliographic details needed to complete each entry. Librarians in twenty-five libraries across Canada also helped by seeking out and interpreting reference sources that were available in their institutions. Happily, after approximately five years' work, the bibliographic material and annotations were ready and the catalogue, *Canadian Children's Books: 1799-1939*, was published in 1992 by the University of British Columbia Library. As Dr. Ruth J. Patrick, University Librarian, stated in her preface, "There is no other catalogue of its range and depth available." Although the National Library of Canada and the Toronto Public Library have larger collections of early Canadian children's books, they have not described nor published them in separate catalogues.

Dr. Patrick also made it clear in her preface that she hoped that the larger collection of early American and British books in Special Collections, in the main donated by the Arkleys, would also be described in a bibliographical catalogue. With the completion of the first catalogue, I returned to my earlier work with the Arkley Collection, this time focusing on the British and American early and historical books owned by UBC. After another five years of work, *Books That Shaped Our Minds: A Bibliographical Catalogue of Selections*

Chiefly from the Arkley Collection of Early and Historical Children's Literature was published in 1998 by the UBC Library. Rather than attempting to develop a comprehensive catalogue of the collection similar to that of the early Canadian books, I designed the catalogue to present an overview of the history of children's literature in English by selecting the most significant and enduring works by genre and time period. Consequently, not only were books of highest literary or artistic merit chosen, but also books that influenced broad trends in publishing up to 1939, the last date of publication in the Arkley Collection. That was also a defining date because so few children's books were published during World War II, and later, due to new printing techniques, books became less bibliographically interesting. The entries are chronological by year of printing except for the extensive section on illustration, which is arranged alphabetically by the names of the illustrators. The catalogue begins with the section "Romance and Legend," and the first entry, dated 1767, is *The Adventures of Robin Hood*. In addition to the bibliographical information and the annotations, each section in the catalogue begins with an introductory discussion of its contents.

Preparing bibliographical catalogues such as *Canadian Children's Books: 1799-1939* and *Books That Shaped Our Minds* is, in part, a commitment to the memory of the people who have donated the books. Collections of historical children's books such as the Arkley Collection, which is the term now used to encompass all of UBC's early children's books, are extremely valuable for three important reasons: (1) they provide access to the original books, which makes independent research and scholarship possible; (2) the chronological arrangement of the materials reveals the roots and early growth of a specific literature; and (3) children's books serve as a record of a society's values at a particular time, with different editions showing the changes in societal values and attitudes that took place over time. For example, the UBC Arkley Collection has at least two early editions of *The History of Little Goody Two-Shoes*. The authorship has always been in dispute, but one edition in the collection was printed for bookseller and publisher John Newbery (1713-1767) in 1765. It is presented as an early "moral tale" typical of the didactic fiction of the late eighteenth and early nineteenth centuries. This edition provides a social history of the times by showing that after the owners became absentee landlords, the poor farmers were forced by the bailiffs or agents of the owner to give them money or an additional share of their crop. A later edition, published in 1804, depicts a very different rural and political background by intimating that everything was wonderful for both rich and poor. The unknown reteller wrote: "Everybody knows that, in this happy country, the poor are to the full as much protected by our excellent laws, as are the highest and the richest nobles in the land."

Maria Edgeworth (1767-1849) was one of the most powerful forces in the spread of the moral tale in the nineteenth century. She was an avid disciple of Rousseau, who promoted realism over imagination, and one of her most popular works was *The Parent's Assistant*, a collection of didactic tales, including her best known, "The Purple Jar." In this story readers are introduced to Rosamond, in my opinion the first real, child-like child in stories written for children up to that time. Rosamond was refreshingly different from the priggish little girls of the late 1700s such as Goody Two-Shoes and Primrose Prettyface.

Another example of a change in societal attitudes is found in different editions of Mary Martha Sherwood's (1775-1851) *The History of the Fairchild Family*, beginning with one published in 1818. This edition contains the famous "gibbet scene" in which a well-to-do father comes home to find his four children quarrelling. He makes them pray and confess their sins and in the evening takes them to where a body is hanging from a gallows and tells them that this is what happens when you quarrel with your brothers. Not surprisingly, this scene was extremely frightening to children and was deleted from later editions, having been deemed too gruesome an object lesson even for the evangelical moralists of the time.

In addition to my volunteer work at the library, the years following my retirement filled with invited talks, conferences and awards of one kind or another. In 1983 I received both the Landau Award for "Excellence in Teaching Children's and Young Adult Literature" and the Claude Aubry Award. The following year, during a British Columbia Library Association luncheon at which I had been invited to speak, I was presented with the Helen Gordon Stewart Award, named after the founder of the regional library system in BC. After a bit of a tirade on my part about libraries filling up with inferior books for young people, I was reported as saying, "Let's be clear on one thing. You don't need seven years of university training to hand out Sweet Valley Highs." My comments brought the house down.

In 1987 an annual prize, now sponsored by the BCLA, was established to identify the best BC children's book written in a given year. To my amazement and pleasure the prize was named after me, even though I was told by one member of the committee that this honour was chiefly because I was still alive and able to read and talk about the books. Although I read each book nominated in order to prepare for the announcement of the winner, I am relieved that I have nothing to do with the judging. It has always given me great satisfaction to be able to salute the creativity and skill of our children's authors in British Columbia. The value of my comments on each of the short-listed books was confirmed when one of the nominated authors told me that hearing my praise for her book more than compensated for the fact that she did not win. The giving of the book prizes is a celebratory occasion with the sole purpose of honouring the people who keep our body of quality literature growing, often with difficulty. I was the presenter at the BC Book Prizes evening for the very first announcement of the Sheila A. Egoff Children's Literature Prize, and there coming up to the podium to claim the prize was one of my favourite former students, Sarah Ellis. Her book *The Baby Project* was a first-rate contribution to our small but growing body of contemporary children's literature. What I particularly loved about

The Baby Project was that it is about children and not young adults. Ellis's characters come to life through conversation, with each voice distinct and unique. In combining humour and pathos, comedy and tragedy, *The Baby Project* was unique in Canadian children's literature.

Perhaps due to the considerable success of *Thursday's Child*, I was invited by the ALA to write another book, this time focusing exclusively on fantasy written for young people. My professional writing before and following my retirement had given me the confidence to speak with some authority on the subject, and I was delighted to have the opportunity to focus my research on a favourite genre. Initially I was disappointed that the editor at ALA had structured my material as if it were a textbook, which was not my intention. Fortunately I was permitted to change it into a more accessible and reader-friendly book. It was published by the ALA in 1988 as *Worlds Within: Children's Fantasy from the Middle Ages to Today*. Because I had visited Japan to speak on matters related to children's literature, I was interested to learn that a Japanese translation was published in 1995. The writing of both books with the ALA, *Thursday's Child* and *Worlds Within*, greatly pleased me as I was able to approach books written for young people from a broader, more universal perspective than that allowed me when focusing exclusively on Canadian children's literature.

Negotiations for a third edition of *The Republic of Childhood* began in the late 1980s, I decided, with Oxford and editor Bill Toye, to create a completely new edition, which resulted in my having a co-author, Judith Saltman. To accommodate the exciting explosion of children's authors and books, we added a chapter on science fiction and a greatly enhanced chapter on picturebooks and picture-storybooks. In fact, picturebooks had evolved since 1975 to such an extent that we could have discussed them as if they were separate genres— concept books, animal fantasy, literary fairy tales, poetry picturebooks and picturebooks dealing with realistic everyday experiences. In this third edition, we also chose to begin with an overview of the development of Canadian children's literature, pointing out that Canadian-born writers did not make an appearance until the second half of the nineteenth century, and First Nations and Inuit peoples did not start recording their stories until long after that. *The New Republic of Childhood* was published in 1990 but is now out of print. In my mind, Canadian children's literature has expanded to such a degree in each of the genres that it can no longer be successfully encompassed and discussed in a single overview.

Happily, in November 1993 my brother, George, and his wife, Lou, accompanied me to Washington, D.C., where I had been invited to speak to the members of the Children's Literature Section of the Library of Congress during Children's Book Week. I was deeply concerned that my speech was too long, so rather than go sightseeing with George and Lou, I stayed at the hotel and worked all morning shortening the text. It was fortunate that I deleted much of it, since I realized later that I would have been cut off before I had finished. I was dismayed when we all were ushered out of the Mary Pickford Theater the moment my speech ended, making any follow-up questions and discussion impossible.

A more positive memory of the event was the royal treatment we received at the wonderfully convenient hotel across the street from the Library of Congress. The following day George, Lou and I enjoyed seeing some of the capital city and visiting the impressive Lincoln Memorial and the Vietnam Memorial. My hostess was Sybille A. Jagusch, chief of the Children's Literature Section and editor of my lecture when it was published. As an introduction for the publication, my good friend Sam Rothstein wrote an amusing "histoire" that he titled "Much More Than a Scholar: The Other Parts of Sheila Egoff." *Some Paradoxes to Ponder: The Puzzling and Not Entirely Welcome Development of Children's Literature Since the Nineteen Sixties* was published by the Library of Congress in 1996. I was particularly pleased with the publication as it blended Sam's and my texts with the story and coloured illustrations of an early-twentieth-century

British children's book, *The Story of Snips*. Referring to the wit and playfulness of the story, the editor wrote that it "was chosen to provide what we perceive as the perfect tongue-in-cheek illumination of Dr. Egoff's presentation."

Perhaps the most gratifying of all my recognitions took place in the spring of 1994 when, during a ceremony in Ottawa, I became an Officer of the Order of Canada. Thanks to the efforts of a public librarian, Andrea Deacon, who spearheaded the collecting of letters of support, nationally and internationally, and the dedication of a number of my past students such as Judi Saltman, Kit Pearson and Sarah Ellis, a successful case for my receiving the honour was made. I must immodestly confess that the highlight of the evening for me was standing before Governor General Ray Hnatyshyn and hearing my accomplishments read aloud to the assembled guests. I have always loved beautiful clothes, and the seven-hundred-dollar dress that I bought for the occasion also made me feel particularly special. George told me that I had failed to follow the instructions and did not bow correctly to the Governor General and his wife. I do remember waving to the audience, which likely did not fit with the stated protocol either. It was an important night for children's literature as Dennis Lee also was made an Officer of the Order of Canada. George told me that it was the best buffet dinner he had ever had, but I remember best sitting beside and chatting with the Governor General. The only bit of disappointment for me was that my sister-in-law, Lou, had to miss this special event and wait in the hotel for our return as I was allowed only one guest.

Although I appreciated the many awards and honours that I have received from various universities and organizations, I found it particularly pleasing to have a scholarship established in my name at my own university. In 2001, friends and colleagues honoured me by creating the Sheila Egoff Scholarship in Library and Information Studies. The yearly scholarship of $1,500 is for students in the Masters of Library and Information Studies program, with preference being

*The delicate balance between realistic detail and the
solace of imagination is one that has not been achieved
frequently in the books of the past twenty years.*

—Thursday's Child

given to students who are entering the first year of the program. In a
sentimental way, having a scholarship created in my name reminded
me of the pleasure I felt when I was honoured by my hometown
of Galt by being inducted into the South Waterloo Ontario Hall
of Fame in 1997 and into the Cambridge Ontario Hall of Fame in
1998. The pleasure of this recognition was doubled when my brother
George was honoured in the same way.

I am frequently asked to name my favourite Canadian children's
book or, even worse, my top six favourites. Fortunately I have had the
good sense to avoid answering such questions. I simply say that I have
read so many that it is impossible for me to choose because most fine
books are very different from one another. For example, some I have
liked because they made me feel so Canadian, a feeling I experienced
with Farley Mowat's *Lost in the Barrens,* Jan Hudson's *Sweetgrass* and
Norma Charles's *The Accomplice,* nominee for the Sheila A. Egoff
Children's Literature Prize. I particularly enjoyed *Sweetgrass* because
it draws upon my early enjoyment of First Nations stories and tells,
in quiet, rhythmic prose, the story of a self-reliant, fifteen-year-old
girl who courageously struggles against the restrictive role of women
in her Blackfoot tribe.

Another book, *Jasmin* by Jan Truss, was in many ways unique in
Canadian children's literature in that the protagonist is a sensitive,
capable, grade-six girl rather than the teenage male typically found

*Literature written for the young has always been
strongly social. It reflects, although in miniature, the
manners and mores of a given period in society and, in
particular, those values society deems worthy of trans-
mitting to the next generation.* —Worlds Within:
Children's Fantasy from the Middle Ages to Today

in most survival stories. Jasmin, the oldest of seven children, has far
too much responsibility placed upon her. Because of upsetting incidents at home, she runs away to live in the Alberta wilderness near
her home. Jasmin is a plausible, fully developed character, resourceful
and yet romantic in her appreciation of beautiful things. In a number
of respects, this story made me recall an earlier book, Helen Chetin's
The Lady of the Strawberries, in which a ten-year-old girl living on an
Alberta farm has the responsibility for her younger brother after her
mother cannot adjust to rural life and returns to Toronto. As does
Jasmin, Chetin's story exhibits strong psychological elements, and the
skillful development of a child's internal thoughts made it a remark-
able book for its time.

Another author who broke new ground in the creation of our literature is Jean Little, who introduced the new realism into Canadian
children's literature. Her books, such as *Mama's Going to Buy You a
Mockingbird*, are domestically centred, with urban settings that are
easily identifiable by the 90 percent of us who live close to the United
States border. Without the sentimentality of L.M. Montgomery or
Nellie McClung, her child characters often experience emotional or
physical difficulties, but prove that they are able to cope and even
find the strength to help others. Jean Little's stories are developed
with much simplicity but are not simplistic, which is a special gift
many writers do not have. Other books, like Bernice Thurman

Hunter's Booky series, gave me a feeling of happy nostalgia and were a reflection of my own childhood during the Depression years. The books offer many recognizable situations; for example, the courage of Booky's mother who, like mine, made great sacrifices for her family during those difficult times.

From my extensive reading and research, I now know exactly how to define what I call a worthwhile book—a book that is worth the attention of the young. I describe such a book as very rich, and by that I mean one that offers more than a simple plot or an inadequate version of our history, or is minimal in its exploration of our wild animal life. Such efforts do not qualify as rich. I do not believe that I am narrow in my definition of richness. I can still enjoy an Agatha Christie mystery because it offers me something I had not known before. Children must be exposed to the best books available, in part to equip them to distinguish between the best, which is all too rare, and the worst, which is sadly too prevalent. However, I have never believed that a worthwhile book has to be heavy in its approach. There is nothing heavy about Farley Mowat's *Owls in the Family* nor Linda Bailey's Stevie Diamond mysteries. The children in these books are well portrayed, and the familiar Canadian settings are perfectly incorporated into the stories. Besides, children are as entitled to so-called light reading as adults.

Canadians have not always appreciated or treasured our fine books of the past, and with current publishing practices, many of our best modern children's books will soon be out of print. Too often today, the approach seems to be to publish quickly, get a quick return and move on to a new book. As a consequence, we lack an established core of quality resources to offer to Canadian children. Many recent books deserve the title of modern classic and should be permanently in print. I am sure that many of the books I have mentioned are out of print, such as *Billy Topsail, Sajo and her Beaver People* and all of Catherine Anthony Clark's books except for her first, *The Golden Pine Cone*, which was reprinted several years ago with new but less-than-successful illustrations. All too frequently, publishers fail to provide an enticing cover that is well designed and well drafted and reflects the spirit of the book. They say that you cannot choose a book by its cover, but with so many choices available, books are often chosen that way whether we like to admit it or not.

In general, our children's writers are worthy of more attention and publicity than they receive, despite the fact that more money is available today in prizes and grants. One problem is insufficient reviews of new children's books. Canadian children's literature is brought to the attention of young readers largely through the efforts of children's librarians and teacher-librarians across Canada, whether through school or library programs or through organizations such as the Children's Literature Roundtables across Canada. However, almost thirty years after the first Pacific Rim Conference, during which writers bemoaned the financial difficulties they faced, we still do not have sufficient funding to develop and support our intellectual and literary lives. Consequently it is extremely difficult to nurture the talent of up-and-coming writers and illustrators and to support the custodians of our culture: teachers, librarians and parents.

I now wish to say a few special words of praise about those Canadian writers who have helped form my opinions and who I believe could be considered writers of pivotal books. How do I choose such authors? I ask myself, If I were asked to reread any of these authors' books, would I do so with delight? Would I experience two things: first, a feeling of contentment that I was reading something worthy of my attention and a child's, and second, a feeling of excitement because I know that I will get even more satisfaction from the book on a second reading? Such books have qualities in common with great art, music, scientific discovery or any other creative expression of our world. These writers have shaped and are still shaping children's reading of contemporary books. From among contemporary Canadian books, I have identified a few that I believe are worthy of the term modern-day classic, meaning that they should never be allowed to go out of print. You will have your own favourites. I invite you to add them to this all-too-short list.

In 1978 Monica Hughes appeared on the Canadian children's literature scene with the first of her many science fiction books, *The Tomorrow City.* Using a touchstone theory that I adapted from Lillian Smith, I judge a new publication in a specific genre by one of its most successful forerunners. For example, if I read a new fantasy about children escaping to an imaginary world, I think of C.S. Lewis's Narnia series. If, on the other hand, the book concerns fantasy breaking into the real world, I immediately think of Susan Cooper's *The Dark is Rising* quintet. This approach also works well with Canadian books. When I first read Joan Clark's *The Hand of Robin Squires*, which I deemed to be high adventure, I immediately thought of Stevenson's *Treasure Island,* the epitome of high adventure, and decided that Clark's book was worthy to be given to a child who liked this type of story. When Hughes's *The Keeper of the Isis Light* exploded onto the literary scene, I immediately chose it as my touchstone book for science fiction intended for children. *Keeper* has everything—the breadth of this relatively new literature, a highly original plot, a simple but not simplistic style and a powerful theme dramatizing the fact that people both fear and are suspicious of what they do not understand. It also has a universal set of values that should keep it popular as time goes on. Hughes escaped didacticism, much as C.S. Lewis did when incorporating religious concepts into the Narnia books. Reading Monica Hughes converted me to science fiction, and I have read all of her many books, but none has been as compelling for me as *The Keeper of the Isis Light.* I consider it to be a universal modern classic because it reveals so much about human behaviour.

Monica Hughes's talents were not limited to the realm of science fiction. She was also a master of contemporary realism, as demonstrated by her Governor General's Award-winning book, *Hunter in the Dark*, which astonished me with its insightful portrayal of human relationships. Set in the Alberta wilderness, the story has a strong sense of place and is a powerful and moving combination of great strength and tenderness.

When I first read Brian Doyle's *Angel Square*, I was blown away. I had never read a Canadian book like it, and it confirmed my belief that Canadian writers were capable of writing what I would call a rich book. *Angel Square* has everything: humour—almost slapstick comedy—tenderness and a wonderful Christmas story. If one needs a modern Christmas story to read out loud, the description in *Angel Square* is the best in Canadian children's literature. All of us should believe in Tommy's Christmas-night prayer:

> A nice time.
> That's what I prayed for.
> The prayer might work, I thought.
> Or it might not.
> It was a mystery.

To top it all off, *Angel Square* has a mystery. Tommy imagines himself as Lamont Cranston, "The Shadow," who for many people of my age brings back fond memories of many great radio shows. Tommy, for me the nicest hero in Canadian children's literature, is not just a protagonist; he is an activist. He earns the money for his Christmas presents, helps his friends, falls in love with Margot Lane and helps to solve the mystery of who beat up the father of his Jewish friend.

Brian Doyle's Tommy is first introduced to readers as a young adult in *Up to Low*, set in the Gatineau Hills, which I did not read until after meeting him in *Angel Square*. The story is strong enough in its love and pathos to balance the comical scenes. In describing the extraordinary events of sailing Mean Hughie's coffin home in the storm-tossed canal, with Tommy's father and uncles coming to the rescue, wet cigarettes dangling from their mouths, Tommy sums up the book: "It wasn't funny. I wouldn't say it was funny. But it wasn't sad or horrible either." Just after I had decided that Brian Doyle was the best children's author in Canada, I had the extreme pleasure of reading the works of two of my former students, Kit Pearson and Sarah Ellis.

With the publication of *The Daring Game* in 1986, a new British Columbian writer, Kit Pearson, began making her significant contribution to our books for children. With its feel of a British boarding school story, I found *The Daring Game* very appealing because I grew up loving the British magazine *The Girl's Own Paper*. *The Daring Game* was based on Pearson's own experiences at a Vancouver boarding school and has a distinct Vancouver flavour. The students at Kit's old school have now produced it twice as a musical.

The Daring Game was followed by her time-slip fantasy, *A Handful of Time*. The fantasy was unusual for its time in that it moves back to a recent period, the teenage life of the protagonist's mother. In this book, Pearson was rigorous about time-slip rules. She is a follower of Edith Nesbitt, an author who understood that fantasy is deeply rooted in reality. I have given *A Handful of Time* to dozens of children, and it has always been extremely popular.

Then came Pearson's great success with the War Guest Trilogy— *The Sky is Falling, Looking at the Moon* and *The Lights Go On Again*. I have some background knowledge of war guests, as at the beginning of World War II my two aunts and an uncle had distant relatives in England and invited them to send their three young children over to live in Canada. The British relatives agreed, but at the last minute one child's papers were deemed not to be in order, and the family decided that they would all go together or not go at all. They were to have sailed on the *City of Benares*, the ship that was torpedoed during its trip to Canada. That disaster brought an end to the war-guest program.

Pearson's fictional trilogy has both a happier beginning and a more disastrous ending than my story of war guests and deservedly has a tremendous appeal for Canadians, both children and adults. I was at the impressive Kidsbooks bookstore in Vancouver on the evening of the book launch of the third book of the trilogy, *The Lights Go On Again*. The children were lined up out the front door onto the sidewalk, and several of them rushed up to me with great excitement and trepidation asking, "Should the author have let the parents die?" I was only able to answer weakly, "There's the author. Go and ask her." I think I realized for the first time that night Kit Pearson's ability to make a link with the young. Her genius lies in her ability to take very ordinary children and make them interesting, plausible people we care about. Her character Nora resonates with characters in books such as *The Secret Garden* and *Swallows and Amazons*. As her readers made apparent to me that night, Pearson has the ability to write strong surprise endings as she did in *The Lights Go On Again* and in her novel, *Awake and Dreaming*, when a graveyard ghost seems to take over the story.

Awake and Dreaming, her latest novel and winner of the Governor General's Award, shows her firm hold on reality while dealing with fantasy. She also provides such accurate geographic details I actually feel I am experiencing the landscape.

> Beyond them was a tossing kaleidoscope of water and
> land and sky. The huge boat was making its way toward
> a channel between two rocky islands studded with firs
> and small houses. The sea was almost the same grey-blue
> as the sky; fishing boats bobbed on its swelling surface.

I have been a great lover of ghost stories for most of my life. In this novel, though, I think that the blending of the supernatural with everyday life is brought to an especially meaningful fruition. In this case, Pearson actually leads regular expeditions into the graveyard in Victoria in which the ghost lives and where the story takes place! The popularity of this book shows that children want something in their reading beyond ordinary, everyday living.

The most serious error in judging writing for children is to equate simplification with simple-mindedness. The writer for children may paint on a smaller canvas, using fewer and stronger colours, but is an artist still, not merely a craftsman. —Thursday's Child

Sarah Ellis, whom I referred to earlier as the first winner of the Sheila A. Egoff Children's Literature Prize, is another of our outstanding Canadian authors. She is strong on realism, and her books, such as *The Baby Project* and *Pick-Up Sticks*, are examples of her sense of what I would call pure emotional realism. Ellis is interested in developing meaningful relationships among convincing characters, and she does it extremely well. She is primarily a minimalist writer and can put more into a paragraph than Henry James could put onto a page. However, I must confess that I adore Henry James since I love long books. I hope that one of these days Sarah Ellis will write a long book for me.

Ellis's fantasy stories, collected in *Back of Beyond*, are appealing because they are rooted in realism, the basis of fantasy. Take, for example, the first story, "The Tunnel," in *Back of Beyond*. She brings together elements from folklore and the importance of naming (remember Rumplestiltskin?) to the terror of a childhood experience and going to someone's rescue. The story is a piece of perfection. Ellis's later books won even more prizes, including the Governor General's Award for *Pick-Up Sticks*. But none has made as strong an impression upon me as *The Baby Project*.

It is important to mention Sarah's role in the promotion of Canadian children's books. In addition to reviewing for *Quill and Quire*, our professional book-trade publication, she wrote articles and reviews for fourteen years for *The Horn Book,* the world's most prestigious journal of children's-book reviewing. In her column "News from the North," Ellis's insightful commentaries introduced people around the world to many noteworthy Canadian books, authors and illustrators.

Janet Lunn is another author to whom I constantly return. Her *Shadow in Hawthorn Bay* perhaps should not be described as fantasy, and it will not be regarded as such by those who believe in Scottish second sight. Whatever descriptive term is used, it is an excellent novel with a wide appeal. It skillfully combines history (the United Empire Loyalists in Ontario) with the personal struggle of the heroine to rid herself of her Scottish past and belong to the New World. Here again is a successful fantasy that is not only a combination of fantasy and reality, but also has the supernatural world impinging upon the realistic world of everyday life, as in Lunn's earlier *Double Spell.*

When I learned that Janet Lunn had been involved in writing *The Story of Canada* for young people, I rushed out and bought three copies for appropriately aged children before reading it myself. I knew that Janet Lunn is always brilliant and that she would be able to capture the vitality of our history. The book has pleased me as much as an adult as it has any young person with whom I have shared it. Even by just dipping into the book, readers become immediately aware that Canadian history is not dull, an unfortunate assumption that has plagued our knowledge of our own country. I feel strongly that *The Story of Canada* should never go out of print.

I first came across the works of Tim Wynne-Jones through his book of short stories, *Some of the Kinder Planets.* I have a passion for short stories. I have spent a lifetime reading them, from Rudyard Kipling to Somerset Maugham to the Russians to Katherine Anne Porter and Katherine Mansfield, and I carry this interest to stories written for the young. The great value of a book of short stories is that it can offer such a spread of themes, writing styles and characterization in a short space of time.

The difference between literature for children and that for adults was in the nature of the audience, not the character or quality of the material. —One Ocean Touching: Papers from the first Pacific Rim Conference on Children's Literature.

I am greatly impressed with Wynne-Jones's ability to write what I call a combined story. By that I mean a story that has something in it for everybody: realistic setting, wonderful characters, memorable imagery, an unusual plot and a dramatic ending. The title story, for example, would appeal to a wide range of readers. The background, which is one of the author's strong points, is well delineated without being a travel guide. The story reflects his extensive reading of children's books while giving his readers his own literary surprises.

Wynne-Jones's literary strengths are also apparent in his young adult novel *The Maestro*, which, while probably written for teenagers, appeals to a wide range of readers, as do his other books. Initially I thought I was reading a rather ordinary teenage novel with its dysfunctional family and alienated fourteen-year-old. However Wynne-Jones soon turns the story away from the usual, with the runaway protagonist meeting a famous pianist in a completely nondescript cabin and virtually forcing him out of his own hideaway. Now there's a plot. Perhaps young people will not be aware of the identity of one of the main characters in the book, but those used to musical eccentricity will recognize that the pianist is Canada's own Glenn Gould, who indeed loved the wilderness for its ability to offer both solitude and comfort. In many ways *The Maestro* is as brilliant a book as Brian Doyle's *Angel Square,* and yet both these talented writers have sometimes left me worrying about a lack of plausibility in their realistic stories. In *Angel*

Square, for example, I had trouble accepting the notion that a non-Catholic altar boy would be paid for serving on the altar, while in *The Maestro* I found it difficult to imagine a famous musician, no matter how eccentric, going off and leaving the only copy of his manuscript in a cabin inhabited by a fourteen-year-old boy.

The number of Canadian picturebooks that I have appreciated is so large that it is difficult to give them the praise they deserve in a brief commentary. I particularly remember *The Very Last First Time*, written by Jan Andrews and illustrated by Ian Wallace, because of its accurate but surprising circumstance of the tides, salt water and ice in Ungava Bay, an inlet in northern Quebec. As the young girl walks on the ocean floor under a layer of ice to collect mussels, I realized for the first time that salt water could freeze. I also experienced a new awareness upon reading Michael Kusagak's *Baseball Bats for Christmas*, illustrated by Vladyana Kyrkorka, which gives an intimate look at childhood in the Repulse Bay area. As no trees grow there, residents were given trees for Christmas, and, following the festivities, someone had the wisdom to carve them into baseball bats and baseball, not hockey, became a favourite sport of this northern community. As a southern Ontarian, I thought I knew a lot about baseball and even played girl's softball, but I had never imagined the universal appeal the game would have. I was charmed by this story of the challenges these spirited northern people overcame and by the realization that children everywhere love to play games.

I must mention Barbara Reid's unique technique to create her three-dimensional illustrations in Plasticine, so reminiscent for me of Elizabeth Cleaver's paper collages. Like Cleaver, Reid knows how to handle her medium with simplicity, genius and humour, as in *Have You Seen Birds?*, *Effie* and her nursery-rhyme collection, *Sing a Song of Mother Goose*. Her use of a form of child's modelling clay makes her work immediately appealing and accessible to children.

I do not remember when I had my first taste of pizza, but I do know that I was entranced when Dayal Kaur Khalsa's *How Pizza Came to*

Our Town appeared in 1989. The story is set in a small Canadian town. The characterization of the Italian woman who brought her rolling pin with her from Italy melds with the story of the four little girls who become fond of her, making for a very happy picture book complete with a trip to the library to discover the meaning of the word pizza. I still smell pizza every time I think of *How Pizza Came to Our Town.*

Even the simple childlike books that Tundra published have exceptional qualities, both in text and illustration. *Have You Seen Josephine?* by Stéphane Poulin is reminiscent of a cumulative folktale with its repetition and the mnemonic device of repeating the phrase "Have you seen Josephine?" Its Montreal scenes confirm that picturebooks are an effective medium for extending children's view and knowledge of a specific place in the world. For example, children are enriched by experiencing the setting of the Boston Common in McCloskey's *Make Way for Ducklings*, the Paris of Bemelman's Madeline series and the Canadian Yukon of Ted Harrison's *Children of the Yukon.*

Tundra Books has developed a reputation for combining Canadianism with artistic quality. A number of picturebooks published elsewhere, such as many of those by Robert Munsch, while appealing enough at first are, in my opinion, really quite disposable. They provide a moment's amusement, but many have no uniquely Canadian vitality or fine art work, which I believe are indispensable in the literary life of a young child. However, I really like Munsch's *The Paperbag Princess*, which my library student volunteers and I performed as a puppet play many times. One of the greatest books published by Tundra Books was *The Killick.* Written and illustrated by Geoff Butler, it presents an episode of modern life in Newfoundland and won the Ruth Schwarz Children's Book Award. Memories of my earlier reading of Sir Wilfred Grenfell's *Adrift on an Ice Pan* and James Houston's *Tikta'liktak* came flooding back. The plot concerns a grandfather and his grandson caught adrift on an ice floe during a fierce storm and forced to take shelter under their boat. I have not spent much time in Newfoundland, but this book still represents much of what I have learned about the Newfoundlanders, especially from two library-school students who, as I did, defended the yearly seal hunt because it provided a livelihood for the men deprived of the cod fishery.

A newer picturebook star on my horizon is Nan Gregory, beginning with *How Smudge Came*, illustrated by Ron Lightburn, which I consider to be one of Canada's most important modern picturebooks. When I opened it casually, I saw a picture of a young woman who I knew immediately was mentally challenged. It seemed remarkable to me that an illustrator could create this impression so subtly. Then I turned to the first page and began reading, "If there's one thing Cindy knows, this is no place for a puppy. Up goes the puppy, tucked into her bag. Home goes Cindy." I thought that the writing was unusually brilliant for a picturebook. For example, *Make Way for Ducklings* by Robert McCloskey is pleasant but not brilliant. My only comparison for brilliance would be Maurice Sendak's *Where the Wild Things Are*, which took him ten years to write.

Nan Gregory's second book was *Wild Girl and Gran*, again illustrated by Ron Lightburn. This is a picture-storybook rather than a picturebook. Usually picture-storybooks are taken from the oral tradition and re-illustrated. I have always regarded Seuss's *The 500 Hats of Bartholomew Cubbins* as the perfect picture-storybook. In my opinion, no Canadian has ever matched *The 500 Hats*, but *Wild Girl and Gran* comes very close.

Gregory's picturebook *Amber Waiting*, illustrated by Kady MacDonald Denton, has a modern theme—a very young child of a single parent waiting to be picked up from school. Amber feels she is always waiting and weaves in her mind a little plot of how she would keep her father waiting. Like *How Smudge Came*, *Amber Waiting* is a little piece of perfection.

Although I have worn eyeglasses since I was ten years old, I began to realize around 2000 that my sight was failing rapidly. By 2003, even my reading machine was of little use to me and I began dictating this book to Kathryn Shoemaker, who began working with me as a research assistant. Then, because my sight continued to fail, Wendy Sutton agreed to become my co-author and contributor to this book. Not being able to read or write, and depending on others to be my "eyes," changed my life completely. Because I have always been independent, I found being completely dependent on others very difficult. For example, to help me prepare for the presentation of the 2004 Sheila A. Egoff Children's Literature Prize, UBC library students took turns reading the five nominated books to me so that I could prepare my notes, something that two years earlier I had done for myself. I must confess that it proved very tiring to have to listen attentively for long periods. I always used to do my own research, usually by prowling in the stacks of the library, but now must ask others to locate material for me. I also now realize how much I appreciated being able to use the computer. I wrote my book on fantasy, *Worlds Within*, completely on the computer, and completed my revisions and corrections on the computer as well. However, what I miss most is the unique and personal pleasure provided by reading. I miss the worlds that reading opened for me and the access to the voices and perceptions of others it provided.

CHAPTER SEVEN

Till I Can See So Wide

Throughout my career, I have been asked, "What is a children's book?" I have now decided that a children's book is any book that a child is caught enjoying. For that moment the book in the child's hand is a children's book. I had my own childhood love affair with Eaton's Catalogue, a staple of Canadian lives in the early twentieth century. Not having Barbie dolls, we cut out paper dolls from this essential part of our lives. For me at that time, the Eaton's catalogue was a much-loved children's book.

But *this* book is about what, in my opinion, characterizes quality books for children and young adults. The question is too large for a narrow answer. As C.S. Lewis proposed, writing for children can be approached in three ways. He identified two good approaches and one poor one. The poor one is to presume to know what all children want as if they were perfect duplicates of one another. The second approach, which he felt was acceptable, is to write for a particular child with whom the writer has a relationship. Here I salute Lewis Carroll, A.A. Milne, Kenneth Grahame and our own Grey Owl and his *Sajo and Her Beaver People*. Lewis's third and best approach "consists in writing a children's story because a children's story is the best art-form for something you have to say." This is the form, simple but not simplistic, filled with sentiment but not with sentimentality, that has a common touch that guarantees a wide appeal. Many newer books are so narrowly concerned with a particular child's problems that the story does not touch the heart or strike a chord of universality.

For a time, many felt that the mission of children's literature was to link children around the world and thus raise adults who would be able to heal all the world's ills. This once-widespread feeling among experts in children's reading was based upon the belief that fine books would establish a universal bond among young people, promote understanding and rid the world of prejudice, ignorance and intolerance. When the children who read these wonderful books grew up, wars would be outmoded, extreme nationalism despised and cooperation extolled. Unfortunately, it did not happen as hoped; it was mission impossible. As the speaker from South America at the first Pacific Rim Conference stated bluntly, "How can you teach children to read before you can feed and house them?"

Ultimately, children's literature passes adult values to younger generations. Children's literature is written, published and purchased by adults in an attempt to pass on information, experience and values. Since the days of the Puritans, this has been the intention of most sophisticated modern writers for children, although some writers can do it much more entertainingly and delicately than others. For example, I have always felt that the chief genius of *Winnie-the-Pooh* lies in the fact that child readers could feel themselves superior to the rather bumbling animals.

All my life I have had access to information and literature through our public library system. In this country we all pay for other people. I respect other people, and I am willing to pay my share of taxes to support a diversity of needs and interests. I grew up in public libraries, worked in public libraries, taught students to work in public libraries and consider libraries the greatest democratic institutions in the world. If a society were to lose its access to public libraries, it would no longer be a democracy. The Internet has speed and cunning and its place in libraries, but to me there is nothing as rewarding as personal contact and service. I remember the story about a professor who needed to leave his university for a period of time. He recorded his lectures and asked his students to attend class to listen to them. When he returned, he found an empty room and forty tape recorders lined up on desks recording his taped lectures.

I have often asked myself why reading has had such an appeal for me and why I have spent a lifetime trying to convince other people that it is important. I think that it is because each of us is only given one life to live, but reading opens a multitude of lives and worlds from outer space to personal inner space. The ending to Penelope Lively's *The House in Norham Gardens* addresses this view. A young English girl, about fourteen years old, has the considerable task of looking after two great-aunts. In the final paragraph of the story, her great-aunt Susan passes on an important piece of wisdom.

> "It is only those who have never listened who
> find themselves in trouble eventually."
> "Why?"
> "Because it is extremely dull," said Aunt Susan
> tartly, "to grow old with nothing inside your head
> but your own voice. Tedious, to put it mildly."

We all need to hear voices other than our own. Fanaticism is born from listening only to yourself. Reading has helped me with writing, spelling, the organization of material and crossword puzzles, but, most important, reading has given me insight into the minds and lives of other people, often people very different from myself.

Canadian books for the young are now simply too numerous, too good in a literary sense, and too necessary for providing our children with an entry into their own space and time, not to be given pride of place.

—The Children's Reader (Winter 1996-97)

Reading has also given me a great deal of pleasure. Good books give all of us, especially children, entry into worlds that we may never experience personally, and into new aspects of the world we think we know. I am strongly against the theory that it does not matter what children read as long as they read. Let's take this theory to its inevitable conclusion. Would you want them to read nothing but pornography? Would you want them to read nothing but comic books or the Disney interpretations of the folktales? Children should be offered the very best of a wide spectrum of reading. If they reject what is offered to them, perhaps we have not been sensitive enough to their needs or interests. We should provide them with every opportunity to have the best—the best teachers, the best books, the best doctors, the best medicine, the best libraries and, of course, the best librarians.

I have often wondered about the practice of placing mediocre books in libraries. No one expects the Vancouver Symphony Orchestra to choose a poor piece of music deliberately and play it badly. No one expects an art gallery to exhibit a poor piece of art deliberately. Yet libraries are expected to be all things to all people. Is it more democratic to have poor-quality material in libraries if people want it? I certainly have had junk in my life. I have read masses of junk, but at least I found it for myself. Junk is not difficult to find. It surrounds us. To identify the best is quite a different thing. That takes time, trouble and the training of children on the part of parents, librarians and teachers. It takes thoughtfulness and an understanding of children and their interests. The effect of a quality piece of literature upon a reader is not easily understood. Books have to have some holding quality that makes you want to keep turning the pages. I am sure we are all familiar with the expression associated with reading a book, "I just didn't want it to end." You can read such a book several times. My approach is to give children the best first. Then they will recognize the shallow when they encounter it. I have certainly witnessed proof of this theory. For example, one day the first director of the library school, Dr. Samuel Rothstein, came into my office and said, "My daughters are deprived. They have never read a Hardy Boys or a Nancy Drew."

I said, "Sam, I will make sure that they get a Hardy Boys or a Nancy Drew," because I was convinced that I knew what would happen.

I kept my word and when the girls came to return the books, they said, "Are you out of your mind thinking that we would like these books?"

Canadian children's books are better than they have ever been, but most still lack the universal appeal of L.M. Montgomery. Despite her shortcomings as a writer, she struck what can only be described as a common chord with readers around the world. *Anne of Green Gables* belonged to the Edwardian period. In most books at the time, such as Margaret Sidney's *Five Little Peppers and How They Grew* and Gene Stratton Porter's *Girl of the Limberlost*, the chief characters were young lovable girls who finally won over all the crotchety old people around them. Anne did something more. She was plucky, she never gave up, she was gifted at making friends and she was very candid, as confident children are. Above all, she was romantic. Also, I now recognize that it was an asset that Anne grew up along with her readers. Unlike the children in many of today's books, whose problems are so specific and limited that only a few children can identify with them, Anne was an orphan, extremely precocious and self-confident, and ready for any adventure. She had and still has a broad appeal.

Montgomery's flowery writing reflected her love of Prince Edward Island and the romantic style and sentimentality of the Edwardian writers, but it eventually became too flowery for many of her most ardent fans and even for Montgomery herself. As I have said before, naming specific places in books for young people is very important, especially in our huge, anonymous landscape. Canada is not a cozy little country like Great Britain, where paths, hills and lanes have names that date back hundreds of years. Montgomery's books put Prince Edward Island on the map in both geographic and literary terms. Canada has three seas surrounding it, a huge coastline and the longest border with another country in the world. Canadian authors must make our landscapes more recognizable and appreciated, and one way to do that is to describe them specifically in their writing. We need more writers like Catherine Anthony Clark, who featured the BC Kootenay area and its inhabitants in her books. The name "Canada" comes from a First Nations word meaning "the village," but we are no longer a village. We are now an impressively large country, encompassing ten provinces and three territories that deserve to be described more specifically in books for young Canadians.

More good Canadian children's books have probably been published in the last twenty years than in the two centuries before that, but it may be that these recent works lack a link with a world consciousness such as that found in the works of L.M. Montgomery, Ralph Connor and even Nellie McClung. I hope that our modern Canadian authors will resurrect their kind of universal appeal, but it may be that the economic and distribution problems of publishers will defeat such a possibility. Currently many of our books go out of print so quickly they have little time to take their place in the Canadian consciousness, let alone leap onto the world stage. It is amazing to me that the early twentieth century was really the time when we were known around the world, although, ironically, few readers realized that authors such as Connor and Montgomery were Canadian. In the past, publishers depended on the popularity and continued success of their backlists to publish a few new books each year. Just imagine what Macmillan is likely still making out of *Alice's Adventures in Wonderland*. These days publishers are often so busy promoting their frontlist, and books stay on bookstore shelves so briefly, that publishers often let important backlist books go quickly out of print.

You may well ask how reading is any different or any better in these modern times than movies or television. I believe that reading is a much more personal private experience than viewing a movie or television show. When reading a book, one is free to make one's own decisions about what to accept and what not to accept. I have rarely found two people who agree completely about what has taken place in a book. Movies and television draw on the two senses of hearing and sight and provide fully realized images instead of words that we must decode. Thus stories on the screen require us to commit ourselves to the action that we see rather than permitting us to visualize for ourselves. As a child, I never needed illustrations in books, but perhaps illustrations have become more important now that children are bombarded by visual images. Perhaps less-experienced readers would benefit from illustrations, but when young readers find stories that appeal to them, such as J.K. Rowling's popular Harry Potter series, they do not appear to want or need illustrations.

As I have mentioned before, rereading has always given me a greater understanding of the author's intention. The experience of rereading gives me more insight into the characters, themes and emotions such as tenderness and humour. A great book deserves rereading at various stages of life. When children read a book for the first time, they read for the story, the characters and the plot, and they gain valuable experience as readers. Only on rereading do we discover the nuances of the author's style and language. And only on rereading do we find the depth that exists in a book. Reading can be

An author must write for a children's audience, not down to it. The most important single fact, then, that must be understood about children's literature is that it is literature, another branch of the parent stem.

—Thursday's Child

an explosion in one's mind created by "thunderstorms of language" as Brian Moore wrote in *The Pleasures of Reading*. Understanding dawns, deep emotions are felt and readers experience epiphany.

For a young person, a book well worth rereading is Tim Wynne-Jones's *The Maestro*, a book that accepts eccentricity, reveals emotional growth and resolves a young boy's troubled circumstances. Such childhood reading prepares young readers for the full impact and demands of more complex adult reading. Children and adults are free to choose to read Harlequin Romances or the Sweet Valley High series, but readers who limit themselves to such books will not be prepared for or equipped to experience the full impact of great literature. Indeed, all childhood is a preparation for adulthood, and most fine authors of children's books realize this and strive to challenge their young readers.

Many adult books have made a deep impression upon me, such as Tolstoy's *War and Peace*, Dostoyevsky's *Crime and Punishment* and Henry James's *The Golden Bowl*. My preparation for such books began in my childhood when I learned to recognize and understand the levels of meaning, the use of plot, character, narrative structure, metaphor, style and the various forms of literature. My early reading also activated my imagination, my visualization. In my mind I lived with Anna Karenina. I often have had to reread the adult books I read as a child in order to attain their greater depth of meaning.

A reading of fine children's books helps one not only to read fine adult literature, but also to reach a deeper level of understanding of literature and life. I now feel that Graham Greene was a little too dogmatic when he claimed that books have an influence only in childhood. I can still remember when I first read *Anna Karenina* and *War and Peace,* and those books continue to have an impact on me as an adult. I think that Tolstoy's Natasha is one of the most interesting heroines I have met in a book. Within her narrow world, she managed to make a place for herself, as did unforgettable characters in the works of the Brontë sisters and Jane Austen. In my life as a critic of children's literature, I try never to forget that one cannot predict the influence a book will have upon an individual, especially upon a child.

I have often wondered why sociologists have not studied children's books more closely and critically. I have discovered that fine writers for children are successful because they not only recall childhood experiences but also are able to remember their thoughts and feelings when they were children. There is a truthfulness in their depiction and assessment of childhood. Children's books are perhaps the greatest sociological markers or indicators of how a society regards its children at any given time. If you read children's literature as a discipline and trace it through the centuries, you will recognize the literary growth that has taken place and you will appreciate geniuses who have authored the best of our literature for children. Every country has its great children's books: Sweden has Astrid Lindgren's *Pippi Longstocking,* Germany has Erik Kastner's *Emil and the Detectives,* Italy has Collodi's *Pinocchio,* and the United States has Mark Twain's *Adventures of Tom Sawyer* and Louisa May Alcott's *Little Women.* A good children's book need not be a heavy, challenging read. Children need not struggle to come to terms with its content. *Alice's Adventures in Wonderland* may give some children considerable pause, but most of the "good" books, such as Tolkien's *Lord of the Rings,* cross the boundary between the reading of adults and the reading of children, as do most legends and myths and most folklore, and are genuinely accessible to all.

I sense that children's literature has reached a plateau as it has so often done in the past—a catching of the breath, as it were, before it moves on. The young certainly need books of their own time and place, and I recognize that standards, like tastes, are subject to constant shifting. Still, I can only wish that contemporary tastes were not so very bland and utterly "everyday-ish." Where has the idea gone of literature taking us out of ourselves, giving us visions of something beyond the humdrum, getting us excited about language?

—Some Paradoxes to Ponder

I was quite snobbish for a while about what I considered to be good writing. For me, everything had to be as good as George MacDonald's fantasies, Robert Louis Stevenson's high adventure, *Treasure Island*, or C.S. Lewis's *Chronicles of Narnia*. Only later did I realize that content or subject can be as important as style. Content encompassing current events, for example, is more frequently found in realistic fiction, biography or autobiography.

Lillian Boraks-Nemetz's *The Old Brown Suitcase* is an example of the latter. It is a well-written book based on the author's own experience as a Jewish child forced to hide during the Holocaust. Deborah Ellis's *The Breadwinner* is an excellent example of strong, timely, realistic fiction. It has been well received for its interpretation for children of events in Afghanistan in the 1990s. We need more such books for the young, books that raise the reader's awareness of what has gone on and what is going on in the world. *The Breadwinner* is the first book of a trilogy that continues with *Parvana's Journey* and ends with *Mud City*. Each volume takes place in modern Afghanistan and reflects the current struggle, particularly for women and young girls. This series, much like C.S. Lewis's Narnia books, is based on a single premise but has a variety of characters and adventures with each book different in its breadth and scope. Two other fine Canadian novels dealing with contemporary events are James Heneghan's *Torn Away*, linked with the political and religious struggle in Northern Ireland, and William Bell's *Forbidden City*, which is set during the horror of the events that took place in China's Tiananmen Square.

Because Canadian children's literature is relatively new as a body of work, perhaps its progress can be measured in the number of anthologies it has produced. We now have five significant ones, but the first, *Kanata*, compiled by Mary Rubio and Glenys Stow in 1976, is perhaps the closest to its Canadian roots. Its contents, quite rightly, begin with Inuit and First Nations creation legends, such as "How Raven Created the World." It contains the best we had in Canada at that time, such as Ernest Thompson Seton and Charles G.D. Roberts, but also includes more contemporary authors such as Roderick Haig-Brown and James Houston. This collection was followed in 1988 by *The Canadian Children's Treasury*, edited by Janet Lunn, which ranges from First Nations legends to selections from more recent writers such as Monica Hughes and Barbara Smucker.

Published ten years later, Kit Pearson's anthology, *This Land: A Cross-Country Anthology of Canadian Fiction for Young Readers*, has a distinctive structure. Each province is represented by its best-known authors, past and present. The British Columbia chapter features George Clutesi, Julie Lawson, Shirley Sterling and Paul Yee, while the Ontario chapter highlights Tim Wynne-Jones, Janet McNaughton, Brian Doyle, Janet Lunn and Kit herself. But the whole book is a galaxy of stars. It is an excellent book to send abroad or to give as a gift to newcomers to this country.

Tim Wynne-Jones's *Boys' Own: An Anthology of Canadian Fiction for Young Readers* borrows its title from *The Boy's Own Paper*, which was published in England from around 1879 to the 1960s. The Duke of Wellington is purported to have said that the Battle of Waterloo

I have always found it wonderful and true that there is magnificent kindness, perception, and generosity exhibited in children's books. But I realize that these are the qualities exhibited in children themselves, though only, may I add, with the assistance of equally caring, responsible, and generous adults.

—The Children's Reader (Winter 1996)

was won on the playing fields of Eton, and that was the dominant spirit of *The Boy's Own Paper*. Tim Wynne-Jones, on the other hand, is very much up to date with modern stories from many of our finest Canadian writers, stories that rely on interesting personalities and situations rather than team sports and boarding school life. Sarah Ellis's compilation, *Girls' Own: An Anthology of Canadian Fiction for Young Readers,* parallels the *Boys' Own* anthology. I used to be an aficionado of the English weekly magazine *The Girl's Own Paper.* When I was a teenager, I yearned to attend an English girls' boarding school, play grass hockey, get in a little bit of trouble, but not too much, and have everything work out right. In the end, Ellis's selections, like Wynne-Jones's, are not stuck in the past, but represent the best that Canada has to offer both in the form of short stories and of excerpts from some of our many fine Canadian novels.

French Canada is rich in literature, but not all of that literature reaches English Canada in translation. I cannot imagine living without *Maria Chapdelaine,* which I read in translation, *Bonheur d'occasion,* which I read in French, and *Kamouraska,* which I read in both French and English. Perhaps we should have a law that every children's book should be translated automatically as are our government documents. Hang the expense! Children should have the opportunity to learn about one another by reading of childhood experiences taking place in other parts of Canada.

I think Canadian children's literature has a future as long as government support is maintained. All countries, particularly those with small populations, need some form of government assistance in order to sustain a body of literature for the young. We also need publishers who specialize in children's books. Canada is now fortunate to have many literary awards that include monetary prizes that are of great assistance to authors, illustrators and publishers. Many divisions in the world are caused by religion, nationalism, economics, racism, gender and education, but we are all linked by a common ethos of decency. This concept is strongly promoted in the finest literature, especially that written for the young.

I would like to comment on a number of contemporary practices in children's libraries that I find distressing, some of which, such as extending the hours of children's libraries, I have alluded to earlier.

Another trend that I find disturbing is the increase in preschool "storytelling" sessions in which librarians read picturebooks aloud instead of telling stories. You do not need at least five years of university training to hold up and read picturebooks aloud. Library assistants are quite capable of handling that. Unfortunately, true storytelling for children seems to have become a thing of the past.

I am also concerned about the current practice in collection development of ordering only one copy of any particular book. Trained librarians spend a good amount of time reviewing and selecting books they wish to order. If a book is felt to be suitable, at least three copies should be made available, and six copies should be ordered if the book is going to be book-talked with groups. Also related to collection development, I believe that professional children's librarians should have the final say as to which books are to be in the collection. I recall a situation in which a children's librarian felt strongly that library funds should not be spent on books such as the Bobbsey Twins, particularly as they are readily available elsewhere. Unfortunately, when she was absent for a week, she returned to discover that the branch librarian had ordered the very books she felt

*Children's literature continues today to fulfill its ancient
and most important role, that of reflecting society's view
of the young and the young person's view of society. In
spite of a variety of individual situations, there is a fairly
consistent theme that the process of growing up is something difficult, if not fearful. The best of modern writers are not concerned, as were their predecessors, with a
state called childhood, either distinct from or in tandem
with adulthood, but rather with an investigation of those
conundrums of life most evident in the psychological
transition from childhood to adulthood.*

—Only Connect: Readings on
Children's Literature (1996)

were not worth purchasing for the children's collection. Success in
library services is too often determined by circulation figures. In a
desire to increase the circulation, the branch librarian had ordered
series books that he felt would be eagerly chosen by children.

Around the world, Canadians are considered to be conservative,
sensible, non-violent people whether we were born in Canada or
immigrated here. But we are like a family: the children take on the
attitudes of their parents. I think this is why our children's literature,
on the whole, has been rather conservative. I do not want it to be
ordinary. I would like to see Canadian children's books become a little
more fantastical, a little more multicultural, a little more inclusive of
our modern First Nations peoples. Yet as a sensible, peaceful country
with differences that are more superficial than divisive, we need to
make sure that our children's books reflect both our past and our
present. We need to preserve books that have an intrinsic meaning
for Canadians. Unfortunately these older books, such as Grey Owl's

Sajo and her Beaver People, Roderick Haig-Brown's *Whale People* and *Starbuck Valley Winter* and Farley Mowat's *Owls in the Family*, have not been valued and kept available. How many Canadian children today would know about Billy Topsail and his adventures with his dog? I believe that Billy belongs with Anne in the consciousness of Canadian children.

Preserving the best of our children's literature is one of the most important responsibilities that adults must shoulder. Literature and children's books give a heightened sense of life. I think that quality children's literature has a universality, just as childhood does. We think we know all about childhood because we have been through it, but we only know our own personal experience of it. Only a few writers can give us a world vision within the context of childhood, and even that is little more than a glimpse. In the same way we all feel we are experts on education because we have all been to school, but our experiences are inevitably limited and different. It takes a society, or at least a community, to raise children. They take their examples from us, and I have discovered that the young will forgive us adults almost anything. What they really hope for and expect from us is that we have done our best to enable them to have lives that are satisfying and worthwhile. To do that, we must present them with the best that our literatures and cultures have to offer, never settling for mediocrity.

Other Little Children
Shall Bring My Boats Ashore

SHEILA, DEAR SHEILA

by Ronald Hagler

$\mathcal{F}$orty-three years ago, Sheila showed up at the School of Librarianship to join us four other "original" faculty members who were already ensconced.

She insisted on having an office down the back hall with a gorgeous view of the Strait of Georgia, but the two larger ones were already occupied—one of them by me, the very young and brash cataloguing teacher. So she took the tiny, tiny one right next door to mine and stayed there until her retirement.

And, against all odds, she took me into her sphere of interest even though office proximity need not have led to anything more than routine interaction at faculty meetings. Sheila seemed charmed by my genuine claim that I had enjoyed a course in children's literature as much as I had anything else in my library-school studies. She consulted my technical experience in bibliography and, from time to time, requested my pair of younger and sharper eyes to discern a printing technique or an unclear inscription. In return, she shared with me the depth of her literary and societal perceptions.

I came out far ahead in the exchange. Sheila could be a bully, of course: on my own, I never would have engaged in the fascinating exploration of the writing, illustrating, printing and publishing of children's books before the mid-twentieth century that occupied her, and everybody else she could commandeer, for a decade and a half AFTER her supposed "retirement."

Thank you, thank you!!

Dr. Ronald Hagler is Professor Emeritus,
School of Library, Archival and Information
Studies, University of British Columbia.

How Sheila Egoff Changed Her Spots
by Sam Rothstein

*W*hen you wrote about Sheila Egoff, she insisted you put it in the form of a children's story. Thus the last time I related Sheila's career, I made my account into a Horatio Alger story, though without the customary runaway horse and cruel landlord. This time around, I'll try my hand at a "Just So" story, but having by now forgotten everything but the title, I beg indulgence in advance for well-nigh total infidelity to the format.

Once upon a time (I think that I got that right, at least), a library school was just aborning Way Out West. I, the director of the school and also the director and associate director of the UBC Library, had my hands far too full and could expect small help from my colleagues, all of whom were desperately improvising their lectures.

Now, I had already met Sheila Egoff on trips to the Canadian Library Association headquarters, where she worked as a general factotum with particular responsibility for a microfilm project. I saw much more of her in 1960 when she was the person who somehow got everything arranged for the CLA-ALA Joint Conference in

Montreal. I, along with a good many other men, noticed Sheila. Why not? She was good-looking, good-humoured and exceedingly good at whatever she tackled. She was also—and these were key points for me—vivacious, articulate, enthusiastic and very much worth remembering.

And so remember her I did when early in the school's first term I realized that I needed some rescuing. Why did I think of Sheila as the right person to add to our faculty? The answer to that question requires an account of how I chose all of the faculty members for our brand new library school. Some desirable attributes were obvious: of course I wanted people with knowledge, ability and experience. But perhaps even more important, I wanted people who could combat the then prevailing stereotype of library schools as tiresome, boring, narrow and routine-bound. I wanted my colleagues to pass my supreme test: would I myself want to listen to them for fifty minutes at a stretch, three times a week, for a whole year? In short, I wanted colleagues who were keen, fresh, inventive and likely to make an impact. Colleagues like Sheila Egoff.

The denouement approaches. Before contacting Sheila, I ascertained the late-summer weather conditions in Ottawa, where she was still thrashing about in the CLA office. I then telephoned her and said: "How would you like to come out to Vancouver and help the library school? It's seventy degrees, the flowers are still in bloom and kids are running around the libraries." Sheila replied: "It's ninety-five degrees in the shade here, with humidity to match. When does the next plane leave?"

So Sheila's spots changed in an instant as she left managing microfilm to become an executive assistant and instructor at UBC. She did something of everything at first, but her favourite stint was looking after admissions, where our intake for the next year turned out to include an astonishingly high percentage of good-looking men! She also took care of school field trips, danced at every monthly party and, oh yes, taught children's literature.

Well, the later glories were soon to come: rapid advancement to assistant professor, associate professor and full professor (no doctorate needed for Sheila); several landmark books; three honorary degrees and many awards and honours. But all that began with a shining personality and a weather report. And that's how Sheila changed her spots and became a professor at UBC.

Dr. Samuel Rothstein is Professor Emeritus,
School of Library, Archival and Information Studies,
and the first director of the School of Librarianship
established at the University of British Columbia in 1961.

BETTER THAN FRESH AIR

by Janice Douglas

$\mathcal{M}$any will give Sheila Egoff credit for shaping their careers, but none more than I do.

I went into library school after a four-year arts degree, abandoning plans to become a lawyer in order to become a librarian who could work in special libraries or maybe even a law library.

Liberal Arts is just that. I was utterly unprepared for the rigours of librarianship, replete with what seemed like endless boring rules. The Vietnam War was raging, students were protesting all over the world, and we were discussing spaces on a catalogue card!

The one personality who captured my imagination was the chain-smoking storyteller, Professor Sheila Egoff. Her address to the assembled student body was not a lecture but a *story*, a story steeped in folklore and English history told in such a way that you felt you were being let in on an old secret. Not only was the hour fascinating, but it bode well for her classes, which at that time all students were required to take.

Sheila was magic in some ways. She was a terrible namedropper, a wonderful dresser and totally outspoken. She could drink with the troops and let it be known that those troops were expected to rise and shine brightly the morning after (a test at the library school that didn't fit into accreditation). She was a wonderful storyteller, passionate about her field and adamant about giving children only the best.

Without question, she shaped Canadian writing for children even if writers violently disagreed with her. Sheila presented information in class as though we were part of the living story of the evolution of children's literature, and we knew that we would be scorned if we didn't agree with her opinions. Classes were lively with debate from those who had to take the courses but did not care whether Sheila agreed with them or not. She tended to tolerate men better than "recalcitrant" women. For me, her approach was better than fresh air: it was exhilarating.

Knowing better than most the power of story and the power of the campfire and the oral tradition, Sheila put on her own version of a storytelling evening. Rumours abounded about how the evening would unfold, but woe betide you if you did not attend and capture the audience with your own version of a tale. Professors were invited along to set us at ease. We were given tips on how to select a story and how to learn it well, and we were cautioned to pick something simple. I had no idea what to choose other than the works from what seemed a distant childhood. I perused my own collection (it never occurred to me to go to a library or consult with a children's librarian) and chose chapter one of *Winnie-the-Pooh*. It was quite long but a classic, and people would be plied with wine. The story took much longer to commit to memory than I expected. On the day, I even cut my long hair to look more like Christopher Robin and wore some black wellingtons to complete the picture, footwear being a bit of a personal trademark.

The story was fine…although Sheila did comment that it was a little long. I duly graduated and went off to change the world with story.

One of my first tasks as a children's librarian was a preschool storytime. Armed with the fervour of fine literature, I thought I would enliven my small charges with my A.A. Milne rendition. I got nowhere near the end of the chapter before my audience had shrunk to one small child clutching her own precious bear. I had to concede that what had seemed to work with the charm of candles and libidinous academic camaraderie might have to be modified for the less rarified air of public library programs.

Nevertheless, the die was cast. The power of story had been unleashed among us, and we sallied forth like a flotilla of little boats, taking the words and passions of Sheila with us wherever we sailed. And sail we did.

Janice Douglas, director of Youth Services and Programming at the Vancouver Public Library, has worked at the VPL since 1967.

"BE BOLD, BE BOLD"

by Judith Saltman

*N*o single story or image that I can conjure up captures Sheila effectively. She was a woman of many qualities and many intellectual passions: a storyteller, a teacher, a critic and a writer, a mentor to generations of librarians and children's literature lovers.

My first memory of Sheila is from 1970. I was a young library-school student sitting in the big drafty classroom on the eighth floor of UBC's crumbling old Main Library. A delicate, petite, impeccably dressed woman marched briskly to the front of the room and changed my life forever.

When I chose library school over pursuing a Ph.D. in English, I promised one of my English professors that I would not become what she called "one of those smiling girls handing books to children." I said that I was going to work in a rare-books library, no doubt surrounded by Shakespeare folios. But a course in children's literature—something I'd never studied in an English department—

taught by a Professor Egoff—well, I would try it just for fun. I saw it as something to take my mind off cataloguing.

The tiny woman walked to the front of the class and, without a word of preamble, in a deep, still voice began: "Lady Mary was young and Lady Mary was fair. She had more lovers than she could count on the fingers of both hands…Among them all was a certain Mister Fox." After the long story of "Mister Fox," the British folktale variant of "Bluebeard," the refrain left me shivering "Be bold, be bold, but not too bold, lest that your heart's blood should become cold."

And my life was changed. I wanted to be a storyteller. I wanted to work with children. I wanted to immerse myself in the children's books that Sheila introduced to our classes in her rigorous and reso-nant lectures. She taught us the long and complex history and exciting present of children's books: that children's literature was about ideas and spirit; that how something was written was as important as what was said. Sheila taught us that children's librarianship was a calling, a vocation, and that children deserved from libraries and children's books "only the best," her quotation from Walter de la Mare.

Thirty years later, as part of a course, two of my students spent a spring visiting Sheila, talking with her about philosophies of chil-dren's literature and librarianship. One of them said to me, "Judi, you've talked and talked to us about how children deserve the best children's books, but Sheila made me believe it to my core. I will never be the same."

As a teacher and critic, Sheila could always prick a puffed balloon of pretension. Marking my first student essay, she added a brief note: "Please, for me, next time don't add 250 Ibids." And "If you use the word Edenic one more time…" That same sharp eye was still there years later as I worked with Sheila on *The New Republic of Childhood*, sitting long hours at her kitchen table, talking back and forth about individual books and ideas while Sheila wrote in long hand on lined yellow paper. One time I was waxing expansive about a Canadian writer's science fiction story, calling it the greatest multicultural story in all of Canadian children's literature. Sheila fixed me with a stern, ironic look: "I don't believe a word of it. Prove it to me." Or, after I had written a ten-page plot synopsis to convince her of the value of a particular book: "Judi, if you have to write all this to explain it to me, it can't be a good book."

Sheila always treated children's books with great respect and took her writing very seriously. A forceful push for the truth, the courage to never take the easy way out, the energy and commitment that she brought to meticulous revisions of the same chapter over and over, these attributes characterized Sheila's career—her writing, her speeches, her teaching, her criticism. As we reached the completion of *The New Republic of Childhood*, published in 1990, she told me, "Writing is the only thing that lasts."

A professor in the School of Library, Archival and Information Studies at UBC, Judith Saltman is also the author of two children's books and several books about children's literature.

A BOUNDLESS LOVE
by Phyllis Simon

$\mathcal{S}$heila Egoff has had an enormous impact on the lives of countless children's librarians, and that includes me! Although I did not think I wanted to pursue a career in children's librarianship when I was a library student at UBC, I discovered shortly afterward that I had a boundless love for children's literature that eventually led to a career change, thereby altering my future life choices forever! In fact, my very first job after graduation as a part-time, fill-in librarian put me into a panic because I felt wholly unprepared for children's services.

After reading five of Sheila's recommended books (Although this happened in 1973, I still remember the five titles: *Mr. Popper's Penguins*, *The Children of Green Knowe*, *Nightbirds on Nantucket*, *The Cricket in Times Square* and *Tristan and Isolde*), I realized that my life path *had* to include a career in children's librarianship. The next big change I made, the founding of the children's bookstore Kidsbooks, took another ten years. That decision also followed logically from my courses with Sheila and from my public-library work experience. None of this could have happened without Sheila's influence, without the passion for children's literature that she always shared with her students and colleagues.

Phyllis Simon established and operates
Kidsbooks, an outstanding children's bookstore in
Vancouver and North Vancouver, and actively showcases
the work of children's authors and illustrators.

Hydroponic Vegetables
and a Steely Glance
by Sarah Ellis

*I*t all started with Sheila Egoff. She led me to children's literature. Children's literature led me to becoming a children's librarian. Being a children's librarian led me to Simmons College. Simmons College led me to becoming a writer. Being a writer led me to becoming who I am. That, at least, is one way I can trace the path.

Why, then, can I not remember any of her actual classes? I certainly remember Sheila at library school. I remember her roaring down the hall past the student lounge, trailing clouds of glory disguised as cigarette smoke. I remember her sweet-talking some poor unsuspecting cataloguing student into doing the sound recording for our puppet show of Scheherezade. I remember driving with her out to the Fraser Valley somewhere to do storytelling for seniors. I also remember what she wrote on my first paper for her. "Where did you learn this eccentric approach to bibliography?"

I remember sitting at her kitchen table while she kept my wine-glass topped up and read from yellow-lined legal pads and invited comment. I remember her saying in response to several of my comments, "I don't believe a word you're saying." I remember food—baked salmon and roast beef and my first experience of hydroponic tomatoes. I remember sitting in some chaotic office, giddy and giggly with exhaustion, doing last-minute preparations for the Pacific Rim Conference on Children's Literature.

I remember generosity on all fronts. One night after a long evening of editing and imbibing, she tried to give me her living room rug. When I declined she settled for giving me an Italian double-knit dress, so much more suited to her slim and elegant self than to me. I remember her taking a group of us to the William Tell Restaurant and ordering champagne cocktails. She was always giving away books, pressing them upon us. I remember her finding us jobs, part-time work while we were in school and, in my case, my first professional position. I don't know what she said to the Toronto Public Library staff, but they hired me sight unseen without an interview.

With all these memories, where are the memories of class? Where are the Resources for Children and Services to Children classes? I must have been there. They are recorded on my transcript. Besides, I absorbed every tenet of the world according to Sheila: only the best is good enough for children; the bad drives out the good; if you know the history of children's books, then you see that there is nothing new under the sun; the problem novel is not literature. Sheila was tough-minded, widely read, unsentimental and enthusiastic. She thought internationally. She had high standards and she relished controversy. In my working life as a librarian and as a writer, I often feel I come sadly short of applying Sheila's ideals, but I've never been shaken in my belief in them.

But back to my initial question. How did I absorb these ideas when I have no memory of her espousing them? I have a theory. Sheila has always enjoyed an inventive, science-fiction premise, so here's mine: I think Sheila A. Egoff emitted an undetectable mind-altering power. She had a variety of transmission modes—smoke, wine, hydroponic vegetables, a steely glance, a written comment, an act of surreptitious kindness. A few people are immune, but not many. Once you were infected with this power, you were changed for life. I consider it a piece of rare good luck that I was one of the susceptible.

Sarah Ellis is a children's librarian and a Governor General's Award-winning children's author.

The Magic of Story

by Corinne Durston

I first heard about Sheila Egoff
when I arrived in BC to join my boyfriend and to attend library
school in the fall of 1975. Patrick had just finished the first year of the
library school program, and I was eager to begin exploring courses
that would enhance my Canadian history degree. We attended and
hosted a number of parties that summer where I heard Sheila and
the courses she gave talked about in glowing terms.

When I began the core courses in the fall, I would see Sheila flying
down the hall with her keys rattling around her neck. She was always
stylish, her clothes striking and wonderfully, wondrously unusual and
colourful. Over the course of that gruelling first year, the talk about
her classes and her personality piqued my interest and curiosity. That
summer I read my way through her various reading lists, recapturing
my childhood as I did so. I discovered authors heretofore unknown
to me such as Alan Garner, Susan Cooper, Ursula Le Guin, to name
but a few. I also reacquainted myself with favourite works, such as

Peter Pan, *The Secret Garden*, *Wind in the Willows* and C.S. Lewis's seven Narnia books. The experience lured me away from Advanced Reference, and I enrolled in Children's Services and Literature at the beginning of second year.

Weeks before the second-year courses were to begin, I gave birth to my second daughter. Sheila and Margaret Burke arrived on our doorstep laden with a gigantic cooked roast beef and flagons of wine. In addition, Sheila insisted that the newborn, Chloe Alexis, was welcome to attend classes with me. As I was breast-feeding and anxious to be with my three-week-old infant, Sheila's generous invitation was an unbelievable relief.

That school year was one of discovery, exploration and a prescient introduction to the flowering of Canadian children's literature that was just beginning to blossom. As author of the second edition of *The Republic of Childhood*, which had been published the previous year in 1975, Sheila infused each and every class with the breadth and depth of her knowledge. Her lectures were a heady mix of vigorous debate, entrancing storytelling (time and time again, Sheila would demonstrate her awe-inspiring skills) and stories about her friends in Canadian literary circles such as William Toye and Elizabeth Cleaver.

In Sheila's Children's Services classes, we developed puppet scripts, practised book talking and learned to tell stories. These stories were told in classes held at Sheila's apartment where Sheila fed us well and gave us wonderful wine to drink. For those of us on student allowances, the food and wine seemed far beyond the quality we normally consumed. The nervousness we all felt when it was our turn to tell the story we had so carefully selected fell away as we began to understand the magic of story and the power of "three." Sheila taught us to feel the rhythm of language of the age-old common stories told by so many cultures and to appreciate the repetition that made the stories so powerful when heard. The excitement of finding a new author and discussing how children would react to the themes and storyline set the stage for my becoming a children's librarian and later a strong advocate for reader's advisory work with adults.

Along with several others, I was privileged to sit around Sheila's dining room table in the ensuing years as she wrote *Thursday's Child* and *Worlds Within*. We challenged her theories about trends in modern children's literature and fantasy, often arguing late into the night over the remains of dinner and empty wine bottles.

After library school (as it was called when I was a student) ended, I spent almost a year working under Sheila's direction on the Arkley Collection in Special Collections at UBC. Her scholarship and knowledge of historical children's material were vast, and I enjoyed the treasure hunt that occurred each day as we traced the provenance of a work.

For years we attended parties at Sheila's as she continued to spoil her former students. She played bridge with us for many years, and everyone was relieved when she quit smoking.

In the early 1990s, a university student doing a study on mentors who had influenced us interviewed me. Without hesitation I said that Sheila Egoff had had more influence on me and my life's direction than any other person I had encountered. But for her, I likely would have ended up in a university library or archives where I would never have realized the power and importance of story in a child's life.

Corinne Durston is the director of Branches—
West and Technical Services, Vancouver Public Library.

ONLY THE VERY BEST

by Kit Pearson

When I attended the School of Librarianship at UBC, you were not allowed to specialize until the second year. I impatiently bided my time until I could indulge in my reason for going to library school: to take courses from the famous Sheila Egoff. In the meantime, Sheila was my advisor, and sometimes I would shyly talk to her about children's books. She was so encouraging and interested that I was all the more eager to take her courses.

In 1976, during the second year of the program, I finally was able to immerse myself in my passion. This was also the year that Sheila coordinated the first Pacific Rim Conference on Children's Literature. This could not have been a better year to be one of Sheila's students as she enlisted all of us to help. A friend and I were in charge of organizing all the discussion groups, and because Sheila assumed we could do this enormous task, we did! In the second term, I was hired as Sheila's student assistant and was trusted to make booklists for the conference, or casually asked to phone an author in Australia or Britain. For me, the Pacific Rim conference remains the most stimulating and rich one I have ever attended. Being very fond of nice clothes, Sheila bought a whole new wardrobe for the week, but was so busy she ended up wearing the same outfit every day! When our class discovered that Sheila had never had a teddy bear as a child, we bought her one as a present, a lovely English mohair bear. We put it in one of the display cases for the conference, but sadly it mysteriously disappeared, never to be found.

It's impossible to list my many memories of Sheila during that year at library school. Outside of class we had jolly evenings at her apartment, rehearsing stories and puppet shows. I learned of British mystery writers in Sheila's Young Adult Literature course and borrowed books from her extensive collection. My main memory is of continually being under the influence of an amazing mind, one that cared fervently that children be given the very best. We felt we were a privileged group, and we were initiated into a secret: that children's literature is equal to the very best writing in the world. On a warm spring afternoon in the last week of school, our class sat under a tree and listened to Dennis Lee read from his new book of children's poetry. The early tradition of Canadian literature for children, which Sheila recognized in *The Republic of Childhood*, was now blossoming in Lee's innovative and humorous writing.

When I became a children's librarian, I tried very hard to live up to the high standards for excellence in literature that Sheila had inspired. When I became a writer for children, however, this goal was harder to attain. How could I ever write anything that would meet Sheila's ideal—that only the very best was good enough for the young? Of course I never have, but having had Sheila as a teacher has ensured that I will always try. Sheila was a staunch champion of my writing as well as that of other Canadian writers.

One reason for Sheila's success as a teacher was that she always treated us as equals and as friends, and over the years our friendship deepened. When I phoned Sheila to tell her that my first book had been accepted, she ordered me to come over at once; the champagne was open when I arrived. Whenever a visiting author or scholar was in town, Sheila invited a crowd to her home to honour them with one of her bountiful feasts. She was always ready to welcome me, with a glass of wine for me and crackers for my dogs. We would indulge in literary gossip, and I was always awed by the realization that the sharp mind that had impressed me at library school had never dulled.

Kit Pearson is a Governor General's
Award-winning writer for children.

An Ever-Present Inspiration

by Kieran Kealy

I do not believe I am being at all hyperbolic when I suggest that Sheila Egoff was, in many ways, a major force in legitimizing children's literature, and particularly Canadian children's literature, as an academic discipline. Her *Republic of Childhood* not only introduced Canadian children's literature to much of the academic community, but it did so in a way that invited evaluative discussion. She provided not only the necessary encyclopedic coverage of the various genres, but also a precise evaluation of the literary merits of individual works, quite brazenly pointing out where some of even the most revered of texts fell short of her demanding standards. She certainly was the major influence in this medievalist's discovery of an area in which I taught quite happily for over thirty years. And fittingly, it was also her work that ultimately provided me with the opportunity to teach in this area of children's literature.

The UBC English Department in the early 1970s offered a course in children's literature but would not give it credit as a senior course. It simply was not considered worthy of serious academic consideration. But the work of Sheila and other scholars, such as our own department's Susan Wood, demanded that such a policy be re-evaluated and, in the mid-1970s, we finally offered our first course in what has become, certainly in terms of enrolment, one of the department's most successful courses. Sheila's contributions, of course, go well beyond having helped me convince a skeptical department of the value of children's literature. She also helped make UBC a major academic resource for study in this area, as well as inspiring an entire generation of children's writers such as Sarah Ellis and Kit Pearson, who have clearly established Canadian children's literature as a major part of the burgeoning children's literature discipline. I thank Sheila for many things, but what I will always be most grateful for is that it was her work and reputation that made possible the establishment of a course that gave me my happiest moments in my teaching career. To paraphrase P.L. Travers's comment on her Mary Poppins: "There just can't be too many Sheila Egoffs." Alas, there was but one, and I am eternally grateful that I was able to know her as a colleague and ever-present inspiration.

Dr. Kieran Kealy retired in 2005 from
the English Department, University of British Columbia,
where children's literature was among the subjects he taught.

"Come, Sit By Me and Read."

by Nan Gregory

At a meeting of the Children's Writers
and Illustrators of B.C. (CWILL B.C.), circa 2000.

*S*heila speaks eloquently about her concerns regarding what she sees as the lowering of standards for language in children's books. She cites a book where the young hero makes up a word and soon the whole town is using it.

"What sense is that?" she asks.

The gathering is not sympathetic. They are conscious that their own writing would likely not measure up in her eyes. "Society needs new words," someone protests. "What about astronaut, for example?"

"Astronaut comes from the Greek 'astron,' a star, and 'nautes,' sailor. It has meaning. Sailor of the stars. It has roots! It's not nonsense!"

In Sheila's study, April, 2005.

"It's Nan!" I call as I enter the room, unsure her failing eyes will recognize me. I've come to help read Sheila this year's crop of books short-listed for the Egoff award so that she can craft in her head a personal remark on each now that she cannot see to write. She is determined to attend the awards banquet even though in her weakened state she has made it downstairs to her own living room only twice in the last month.

"They've given me three tickets. I have to be there," she says. Knowing she is too frail to make the journey to the podium, she has arranged for a microphone to be brought to her table. Judi Saltman will speak if Sheila cannot manage it herself.

"You don't have to go," I tell her.

She waves her hand dismissively. "Now where were we with that last book? Come sit by me and read."

Nan Gregory is the author of several beloved picturebooks
and has recently had a novel accepted for publication.

A Funny, Wise and Witty Friend
by Kathryn Shoemaker

*W*hen I think of Sheila, I hear her describing her favourites as "rich books," the books she would read over and over at least seven times because they were the best of the best. When I think of the people in my life who have introduced me to rich books, Sheila stands along with Lillian Smith, Paul Hazard and Frances Clarke Sayers, a great quartet of inspiration to many including my mother, Frances Franklin, who gave only the best to her own children and the children who came to her libraries.

In 2001, at the same time that I was applying to the Masters in Children's Literature program at UBC, Kit Pearson was helping Sheila apply for a Canada Council grant to write *Once Upon a Time: My Life with Children's Books;* together they drafted a first chapter and a proposed outline for the book. Then, in 2002, two happy events took place. UBC accepted me as a student, and the Canada Council gave Sheila a grant to hire someone to help her write her book. Unfortunately, Sheila's vision had deteriorated and

could no longer be supported by some of the computer enhance-
ments that she had been using to write her articles and lectures. I
was delighted when Sheila invited me to be her research assistant,
and so began a rich experience for me as she began dictating the
story of her life with books. In addition to recording her words, I
made trips to the Koerner Library at UBC to find the books Sheila
recalled from her youth so that I could read passages to her. As many
of the books she wished to talk about were new to me, the work
also provided me with an intense course in Canadian literature.
For almost two years I spent three mornings a week at Sheila's home.
It was a golden time, a time I loved because I made a new friend, a
funny, wise and witty friend. Actually I made two dear friends because
I also got to know and treasure Tracey Wowk, an extravagantly generous spirit and Sheila's devoted caregiver. There was no doubt that
work sustained Sheila, and Tracey made it possible for Sheila to work.
Upon completion of the first draft, my work with Sheila ended
as she began planning the next stage of the book on its road to
publication with former UBC colleague Wendy Sutton and editor
Maggie de Vries.

Kathryn Shoemaker is a children's author,
an artist and illustrator, and a college instructor.

Books Mentioned

Aiken, Joan. *Nightbirds on Nantucket*, 1966.

Alcott, Louisa May. *Little Women*, 1869.

Allison, Beverly. *Effie*, illus. Barbara Reid, 1990.

Andrews, Jan. *The Very Last First Time*, 1985.

Anonymous. *Tristan and Isolde*, date unknown.

Atwater, Florence, and Richard Atwater.
    Mr. Popper's Penguins, 1938.

Austen, Jane. *Pride and Prejudice*, 1813.

Ballantyne, R.M. *Coral Island*, 1858

—. *The Young Fur Traders*, 1856.

Barbeau, Marius. *The Golden Phoenix
    and other French-Canadian Fairy Tales*, 1958.

Baum, L. Frank. *The Wizard of Oz*, 1900.

Bell, William. *Forbidden City*, 1999.

Bemelmans, Ludwig. *Madeline*, 1939.

Berna, Paul. *A Hundred Million Francs*, 1957.

—. *The Street Musician*, 1956.

Berton, Pierre. *The Golden Trail:
    The Story of the Klondike Gold Rush*, 1954.

Blades, Ann. *Mary of Mile 18*, 1971.

Blume, Judy. *Are You There God? It's Me, Margaret,* 1970.

Boraks-Nemetz, Lillian. *The Old Brown Suitcase,* 1994.

Boston, Lucy M. *The Children of Green Knowe,* 1954.

Brochmann, Elizabeth. *What's the Matter, Girl?,* 1980.

Brontë, Emily. *Wuthering Heights,* 1847.

Bunyan, John. *Pilgrim's Progress,* 1678.

Burgess, Thornton. *The Adventures of Chatterer
    the Red Squirrel,* 1915.

—. *The Adventures of Prickly Porky,* 1916.

Burnett, Frances Hodgson. *Little Lord Fauntleroy,* 1886.

—. *The Secret Garden,* 1888.

—. *A Little Princess,* 1905.

Butler, Geoff. *The Killick,* 1998.

Campbell, Wilfred. *The Oxford Book of Canadian Verse,* 1913.

Carroll, Lewis. *Alice's Adventures in Wonderland,* 1865.

Charles, Norma. *The Accomplice,* 2001.

Chetin, Helen. *The Lady of the Strawberries,* 1978.

Clark, Catherine Anthony. *The Golden Pine Cone,* 1950.

—. *The One-Winged Dragon,* 1955.

Clark, Joan. *The Hand of Robin Squires,* 1977.

Clutesi, George. *Son of Raven, Son of Deer:
    Fables of the Tse-shaht People,* 1967.

Collodi, Carlo. *Pinocchio,* 1883.

Connor, Ralph. *Glengarry School Days,* 1902.

Cooper, Susan. *The Dark is Rising* sequence, 1965-1977.

Culleton, Beatrice. *In Search of April Raintree,* 1983.

De la Roche, Mazo. *Jalna,* 1927.

—. *The Song of Lambert,* 1955.

De Mille, James. *The Boys of Grand Pre School,* 1871.

Dodge, Mary Mapes. *Hans Brinker or the Silver Skates,* 1865.

Dostoevsky, Fyodor. *Crime and Punishment,* 1917.

Doyle, Brian. *Up to Low,* 1982.

—. *Angel Square,* 1984.

Dumas, Alexandre. *The Three Musketeers*, 1844.

—. *Twenty Years After*, 1845.

—. *The Vicomte de Bragelonne*, 1848-50.

Duncan, Norman. *The Adventures of Billy Topsail*, 1906.

Dunham, Mabel. *Kristli's Trees*, 1948.

Edgeworth, Maria. *The Parent's Assistant*, 1818.

Ellis, Deborah. *The Breadwinner*, 2000.

—. *Parvana's Journey*, 2002.

—. *Mud City*, 2003.

Ellis, Sarah. *The Baby Project*, 1986.

—. *Pick-Up Sticks*, 1991.

—. *Back of Beyond: Stories*, 1996.

Ellis, Sarah, ed. *Girls' Own: An Anthology of Canadian Fiction for Young Readers*, 2001.

Fitzhugh, Louise. *Harriet the Spy*, 1964.

George, Jean Craighead. *Julie of the Wolves*, 1980.

Gibbon, Edward. *The History of the Decline and Fall of the Roman Empire*, 1776.

Goldsmith, Oliver, attrib. *The History of Little Goody Two-Shoes*, 1765.

Gordon, R.K. *A Canadian Child's ABC*, 1931.

Grahame, Kenneth. *The Wind in the Willows*, 1908.

Gregory, Nan. *How Smudge Came*, 1995.

—. *Wild Girl and Gran*, 2000.

—. *Amber Waiting*, 2001.

Grenfell, Wilfred. *Adrift on an Ice Pan*, 1908.

Grey Owl [Archibald Belaney]. *The Adventures of Sajo and her Beaver People*, 1935.

Grove, Frederick Phillip. *A Search for America*, 1927.

—. *Our Daily Bread*, 1928.

Haig-Brown, Roderick. *Starbuck Valley Winter*, 1943.

—. *Captain of the Discovery*, 1956.

—. *The Whale People*, 1962.

Harris, Christie. *Once Upon a Totem*, 1963.

—. *You Have to Draw the Line Somewhere*, 1964.

Harrison, Ted. *Children of the Yukon*, 1977.

Hebert, Anne. *Kamouraska*, 1973.

Hémon, Louis. *Maria Chapdelaine*, 1916.

Heneghan, James. *Torn Away*, 2003.

Hinton, S.E. *The Outsiders*, 1967.

Houston, James. *Tikta'liktak: An Eskimo Legend*, 1965.

Howard-Gibbons, Amelia Frances. *An Illustrated Comic Alphabet*, 1858/1966.

Hudson, Jan. *Sweetgrass*, 1984.

Hughes, Monica. *The Tomorrow City*, 1978.

—. *The Keeper of the Isis Light*, 1980.

—. *Hunter in the Dark*, 1982.

Hunter, Bernice Thurman. *That Scatterbrain Booky*, 1981.

—. *With Love from Booky*, 1983.

—. *As Ever, Booky*, 1985.

James, Henry. *The Golden Bowl*, 1909.

Johnson, Pauline. *Legends of Vancouver*, 1911.

Johnston, Julie. *Susanna's Quill*, 2004.

Kastner, Erik. *Emil and the Detectives*, 1930.

Khalsa, Dayal Kaur. *How Pizza Came to Our Town*, 1989.

Kipling, Rudyard. *Stalky and Co.*, 1899.

Kirby, William. *The Golden Dog*, 1877.

Kurelek, William. *Lumberjack*, 1974.

Kusagak, Michael. *Baseball Bats for Christmas*, 1990.

Lambert, J. S. *Franklin of the Arctic*, 1949.

Lanier, Sidney. *The Boy's King Arthur*, 1917.

Laurence, Margaret. *Jason's Quest*, 1970.

Lawrence, D.H. *Sons and Lovers*, 1913.

Lee, Dennis. *Alligator Pie*, 1974.

—. *Nicholas Knock and Other People: Poems*, 1974.

Lewis, C.S. *The Chronicles of Narnia*, 1950-1956.

Lindgren, Astrid. *Pippi Longstocking*, 1945.

Little, Jean. *Mama's Going to Buy You a Mockingbird*, 1984.

Lively, Penelope. *The House in Norham Gardens*, 1974.

Lunn, Janet. *Double Spell*, 1983.

—. *Shadow in Hawthorn Bay*, 1986.

Lunn, Janet, and Christopher Moore. *The Story of Canada*, 1992.

Lunn, Janet, ed. *The Canadian Children's Treasury*, 1988.

MacGregor, Angusine. *The Story of Snips*, 1912.

—. *Canadian Wonder Tales*, 1918.

Macmillan, Cyrus. *Canadian Fairy Tales*, 1922.

Major, Kevin. *Hold Fast*, 1978.

Martin, Carol. *Catharine Parr Traill: Backwoods Pioneer*, 2004.

McCloskey, Robert. *Make Way for Ducklings*, 1941.

McClung, Nellie. *Sowing Seeds in Danny*, 1908.

Melzack, Roland. *The Day Tuk Became a Hunter & Other Eskimo Stories*, 1967.

Milne, A.A. *Winnie-the-Pooh*, 1926.

—. *Now We Are Six*, 1927.

Montgomery, L.M. *Anne of Green Gables*, 1908.

—. *Emily of New Moon*, 1923.

—. *The Blue Castle*, 1926.

Moodie, Susanna. *Roughing It in the Bush*, 1852.

Mowat, Farley. *Lost in the Barrens*, 1956.

—. *Owls in the Family*, 1961.

—. *The Black Joke*, 1962.

—. *Never Cry Wolf*, 1963.

Munsch, Robert. *The Paper Bag Princess*, 1980.

Nichols, Ruth. *A Walk out of the World*, 1969.

—. *The Marrow of the World*, 1972.

O'Dell, Scott. *Island of the Blue Dolphins*, 1960.

Oppenheim, Joanne. *Have You Seen Birds?*, illus. Barbara Reid, 1986.

Parker, Gilbert. *The Seats of the Mighty*, 1896.

Paterson, Katherine. *Bridge to Terabithia*, 1977.

Pearson, Kit. *The Daring Game*, 1986.

—. *The Sky is Falling*, 1989.

—. *Looking at the Moon*, 1991.

—. *The Lights Go On Again*, 1993.

—. *Awake and Dreaming*, 1996.

Pearson, Kit, ed. *This Land: A Cross-Country
    Anthology of Canadian Fiction for Young Readers*, 1998.

Phillipps-Wolley, C. *Gold, Gold in Cariboo! A Story of
    Adventure in British Columbia*, 1894.

Porter, Gene Stratton. *Girl of the Limberlost*, 1909.

Potter, Beatrix. *The Tailor of Gloucester*, 1903.

Poulin, Stéphane. *Have You Seen Josephine?*, 1985.

Pratt, E. J. *The Titanic*, 1935.

Pyle, Howard. *The Merry Adventures of Robin Hood*, 1883.

Ransome, Arthur. *Swallows and Amazons*, 1930.

Rasmussen, Knud. *Intellectual Culture of the
    Iglulik Eskimos*, 1929.

Reid, Barbara. *Sing a Song of Mother Goose*, 1987.

Reid, Dorothy. *Tales of Nanabozho*, 1963.

Richardson, John. *Wacousta*, 1832.

Riley, Louise. *A Train for Tiger Lily*, 1954.

Ross, Sinclair. *As for Me and My House*, 1941.

Rubio, Mary, and Glenys Stow, eds. *Kanata:
    An Anthology of Canadian Children's Literature*, 1976.

Salinger, J.D. *The Catcher in the Rye*, 1951.

Salverson, Laura Goodman. *The Viking Heart*, 1923.

Saunders, Marshall. *Beautiful Joe*, 1894.

Selden, George. *The Cricket in Times Square*, 1970.

Sendak, Maurice. *Where the Wild Things Are*, 1963.

Seuss, Dr. [Theodor S. Geisel]. *The 500 Hats of
    Bartholomew Cubbins*, 1940.

Sewell, Anna. *Black Beauty*, 1877.

Sharp, Edith L. *Nkwala*, 1958.

Sherwood, Martha. *The History of the Fairchild Family*, 1818.

Sidney, Margaret. *Five Little Peppers
    and How They Grew*, 1880.

Smith, Lillian. *The Unreluctant Years*, 1953.

Spyri, Johanna. *Heidi*, 1891.

Stevenson, Robert Louis. *Treasure Island*, 1883.

—. *A Child's Garden of Verses*, 1906.

Sutcliff, Rosemary. *The Eagle of the Ninth*, 1954.

Tolkien, J.R.R. *The Hobbit*, 1937.

—. *The Lord of the Rings* triology, 1954-1955.

Tolstoy, Leo. *War and Peace*, 1865-1869.

—. *Anna Karenina*, 1877.

Toye, William. *How Summer Came to Canada*,
    illus. Elizabeth Cleaver, 1969.

—. *The Mountain Goats of Temlaham*,
    illus. Elizabeth Cleaver, 1969.

Toye, William, ed. *The Oxford Companion to
    Canadian Literature*, 1983.

Traill, Catharine Parr. *Canadian Crusoes:
    A Tale of the Rice Lake Plains*, 1852.

Truss, Jan. *Jasmin*, 1982.

Twain, Mark. *The Adventures of Tom Sawyer*, 1876.

—. *The Adventures of Huckleberry Finn*, 1885.

Undset, Sigrid. *Kristin Lavransdatter*, 1930.

Verne, Jules. *Twenty Thousand Leagues under the Sea*, 1873.

Wells, H.G. *The War of the Worlds*, 1898.

White, E.B. *Charlotte's Web*, 1952.

Wynne-Jones, Tim. *Some of the Kinder Planets*, 1993.

—. *The Maestro*, 1995.

Wynne-Jones, Tim, ed. *Boys' Own: An Anthology
    of Canadian Fiction for Young Readers*, 2001.

Wyss, Johann Rudolf. *Swiss Family Robinson*, 1940.

Zindel, Paul. *The Pigman*, 1968.

$\mathcal{S}$heila Egoff discovered the public library in her hometown of Galt, Ontario, at age eight, in 1926. Her love of books extended to a life devoted to the promotion of children's literature and librarianship. Sheila was the first curator of the famous Osborne Collection of Early Children's Books, which she was also partly responsible for bringing to Canada. In 1962, she moved west to help set up the library school at the University of British Columbia. Sheila was the author of many important books about children's literature. To the great sadness of many, she died in Vancouver on May 22, 2005, in her eighty-eighth year, just as revisions were being completed on *Once Upon a Time*.

$\mathcal{W}$endy K. Sutton, professor emerita, taught both elementary and secondary school before joining the Department of Language and Literacy Education at UBC where she specialized in children's and young adult literature. Still active at the university, she is now retired and serves as a language arts/children's literature consultant. She also co-authored *The Gift of Reading* with David Bouchard, published by Orca. Wendy lives and works in Vancouver, British Columbia.

PHOTO CREDITS

1. The *Cambridge Times*, Cambridge, Ontario
2. Egoff family collection
3. Courtesy of Toronto Public Library, Archives, Boys and Girls House, Osborne Collection of Early Children's Books, Toronto Public Library
4. Courtesy of Toronto Public Library, Archives, Boys and Girls House, Osborne Collection of Early Children's Books, Toronto Public Library
5. Courtesy of Toronto Public Library, Archives, Boys and Girls House, Osborne Collection of Early Children's Books, Toronto Public Library
6. Egoff family collection
7. Egoff family collection
8. Egoff family collection
9. Egoff family collection
10. University of British Columbia Archives [UBC 1.1/16002-2]
11. University of British Columbia Archives [UBC 70.1/22-3]
12. University of British Columbia Archives [UBC 69.1/4-4]
13. University of British Columbia Archives [UBC 70.1/5-6]
14. University of British Columbia Archives [UBC 69.1/55]
15. University of British Columbia Archives [UBC 1.1/16437]
16. Egoff family collection
17. Wendy K. Sutton
18. University of British Columbia Archives [UBC 69.1/30]
19. Kit Pearson collection
20. Egoff family collection

Author photo credits:
Sheila Egoff: Diane Jarvis Jones
Wendy K. Sutton: Wendy K. Sutton collection